Musical Instrument
And musical note Coloring Book
For kids

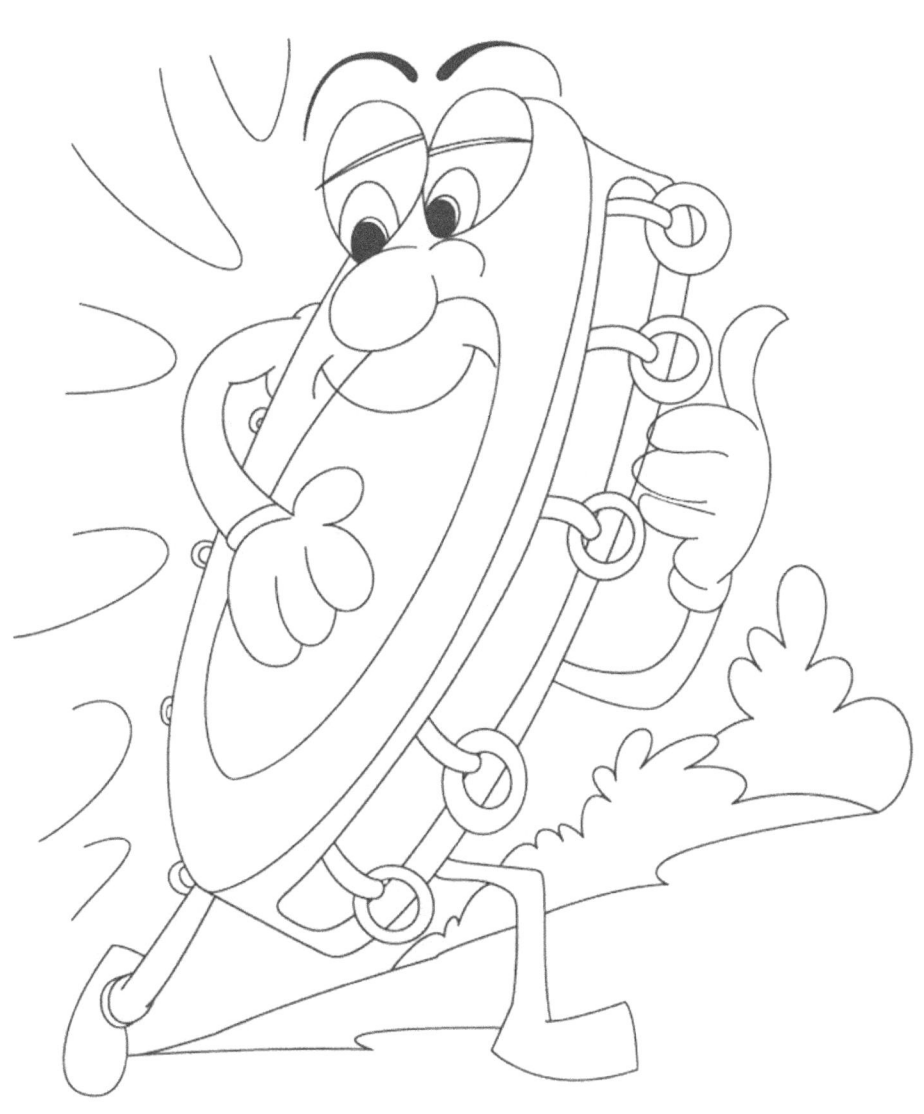

Musical Instrument
And musical note
Coloring Book

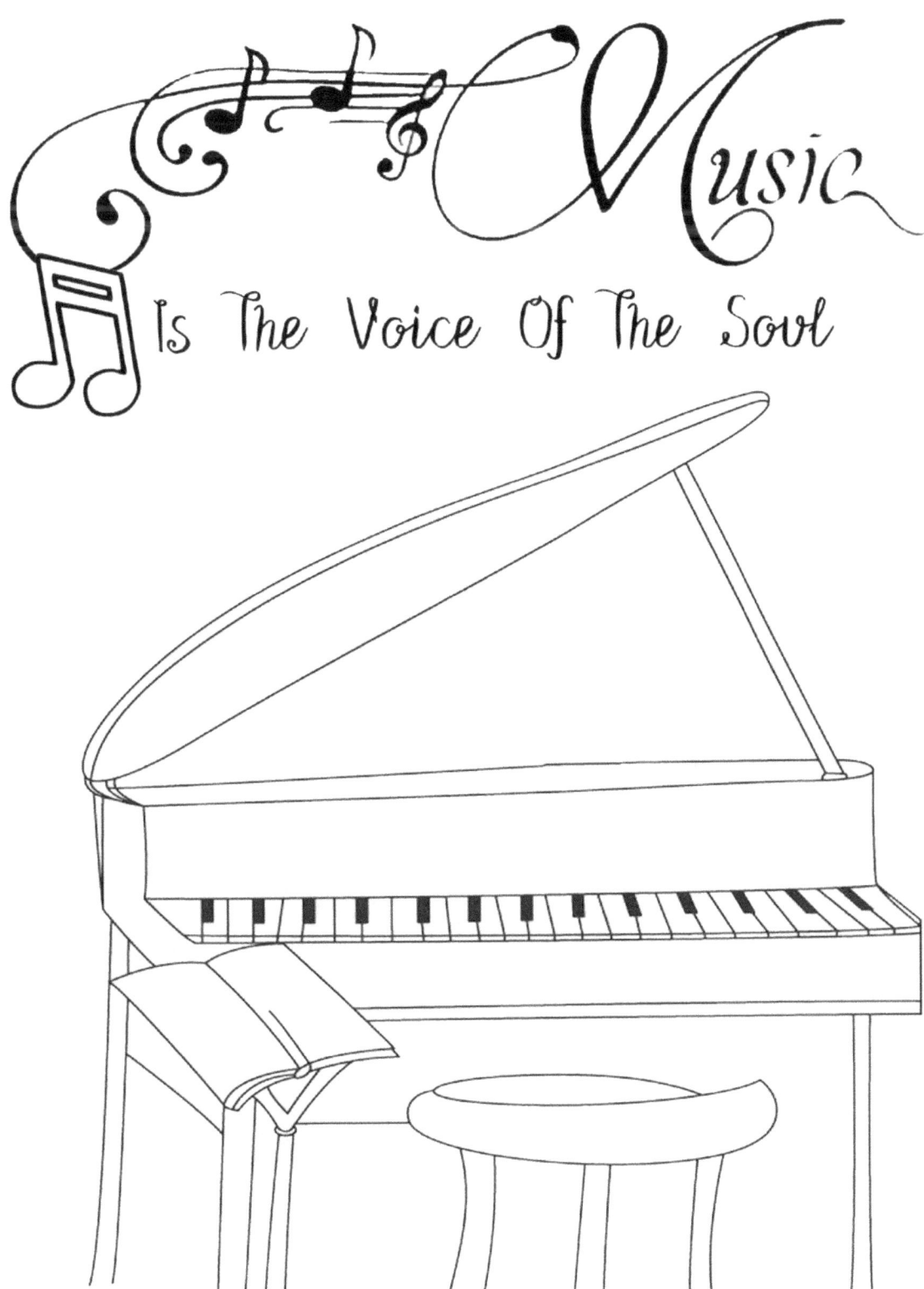

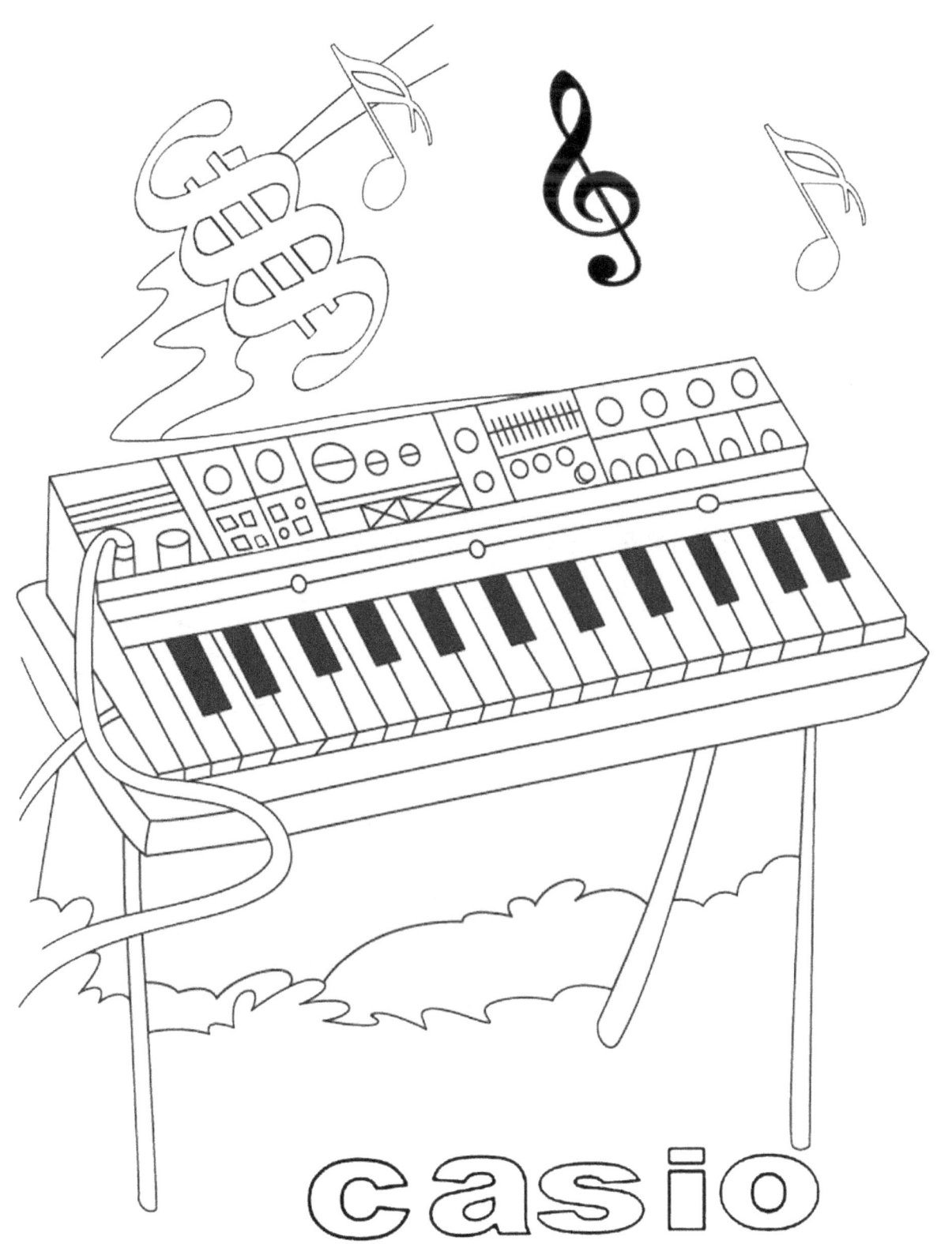

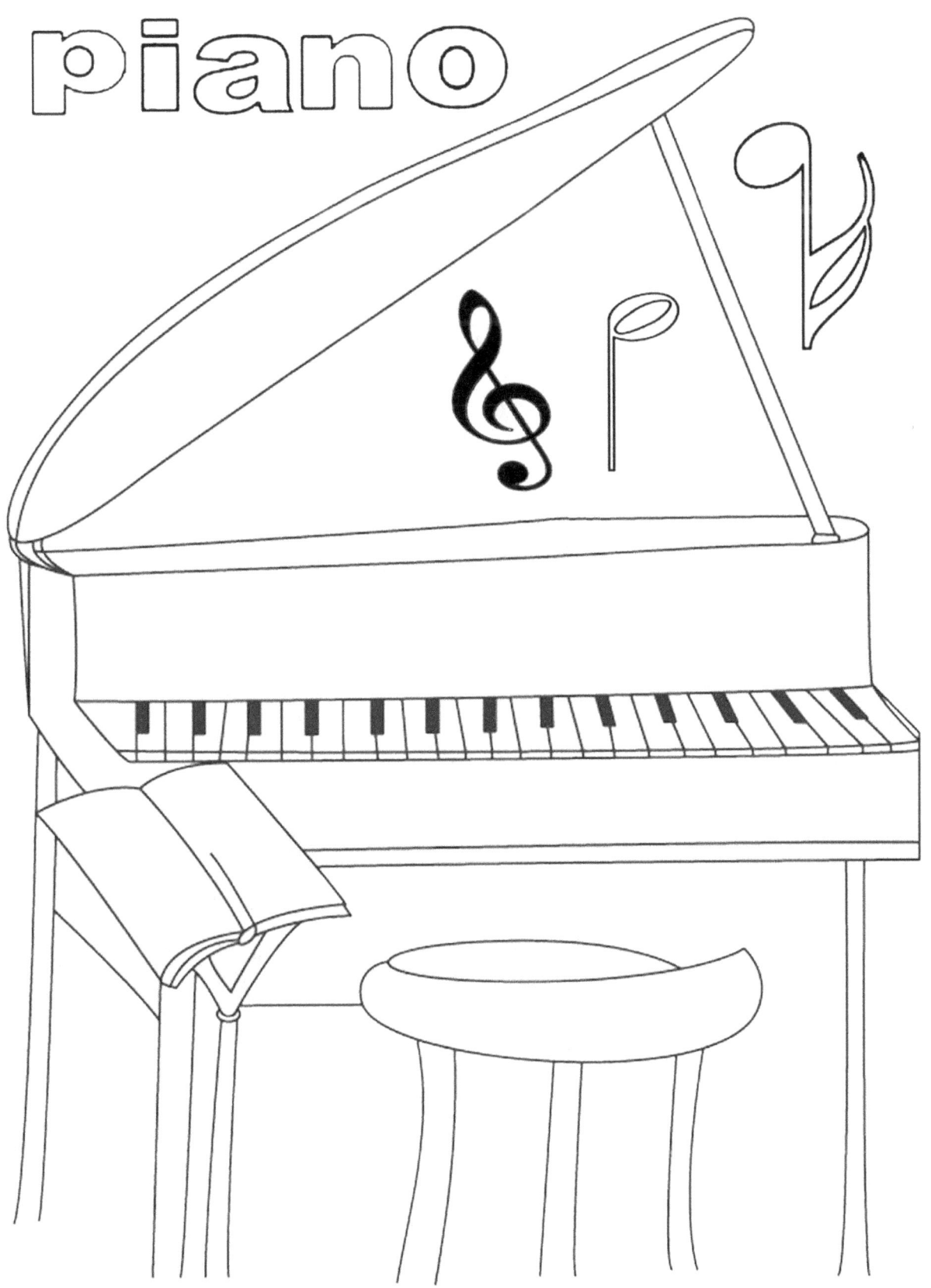

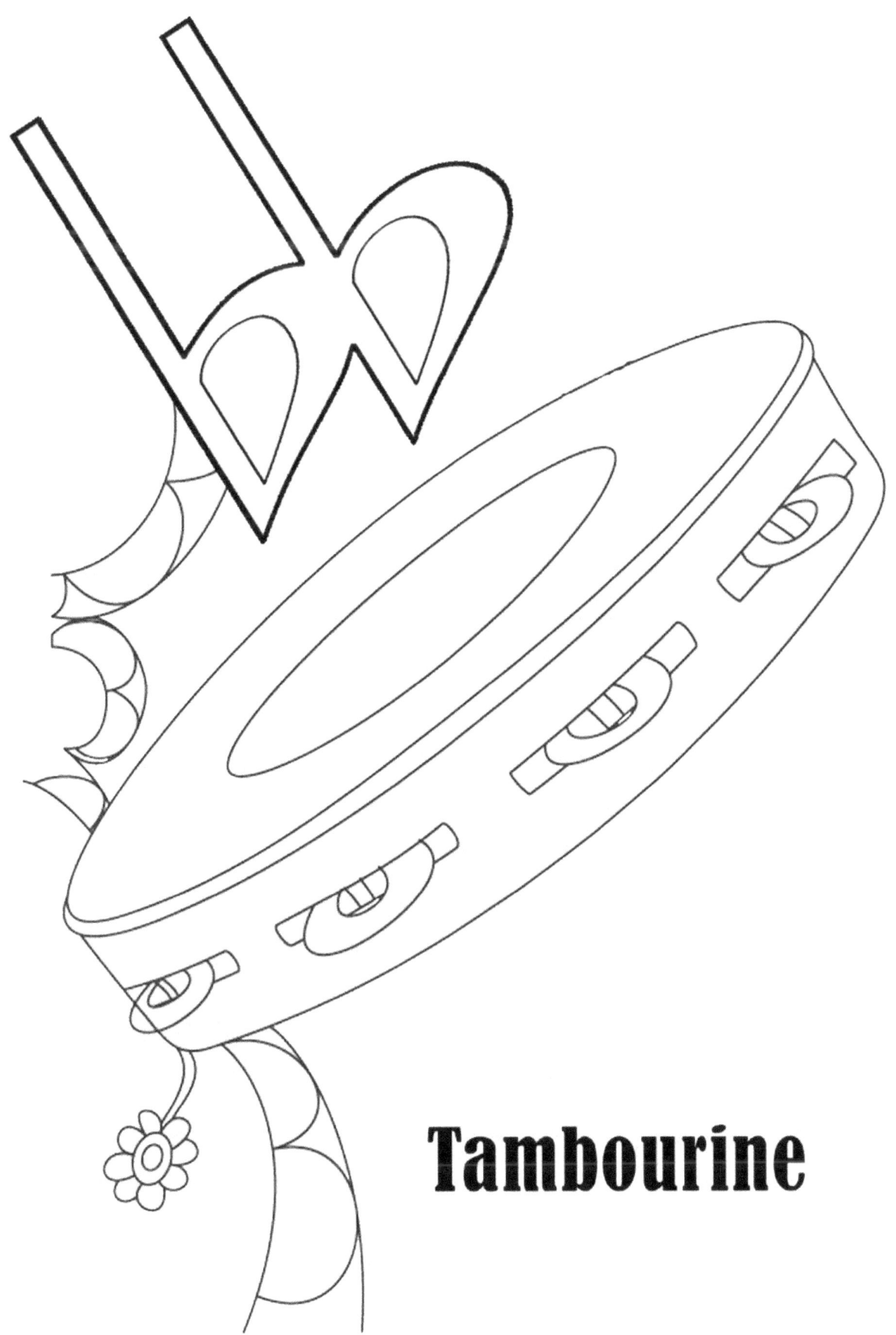

Tambourine

Maracas

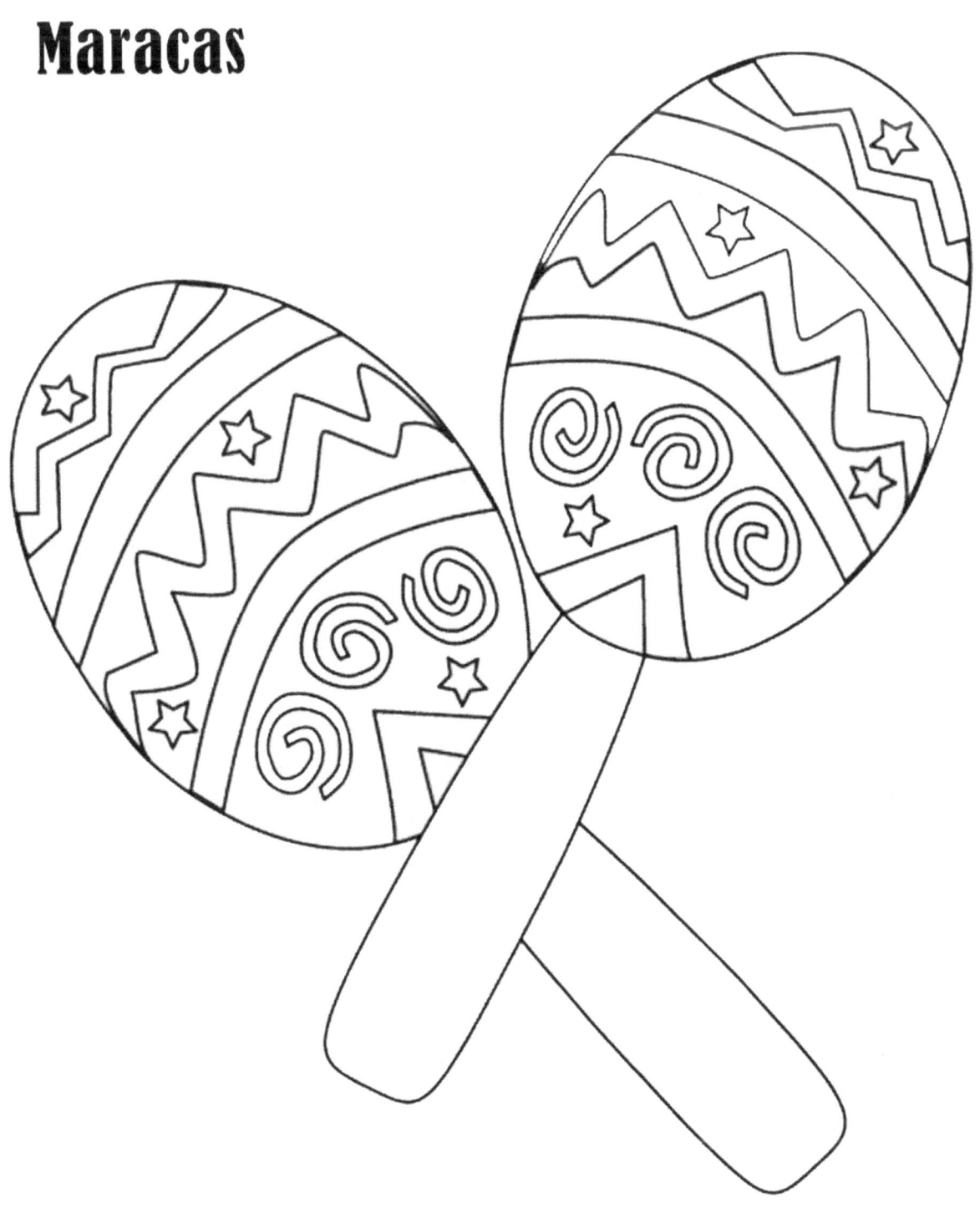

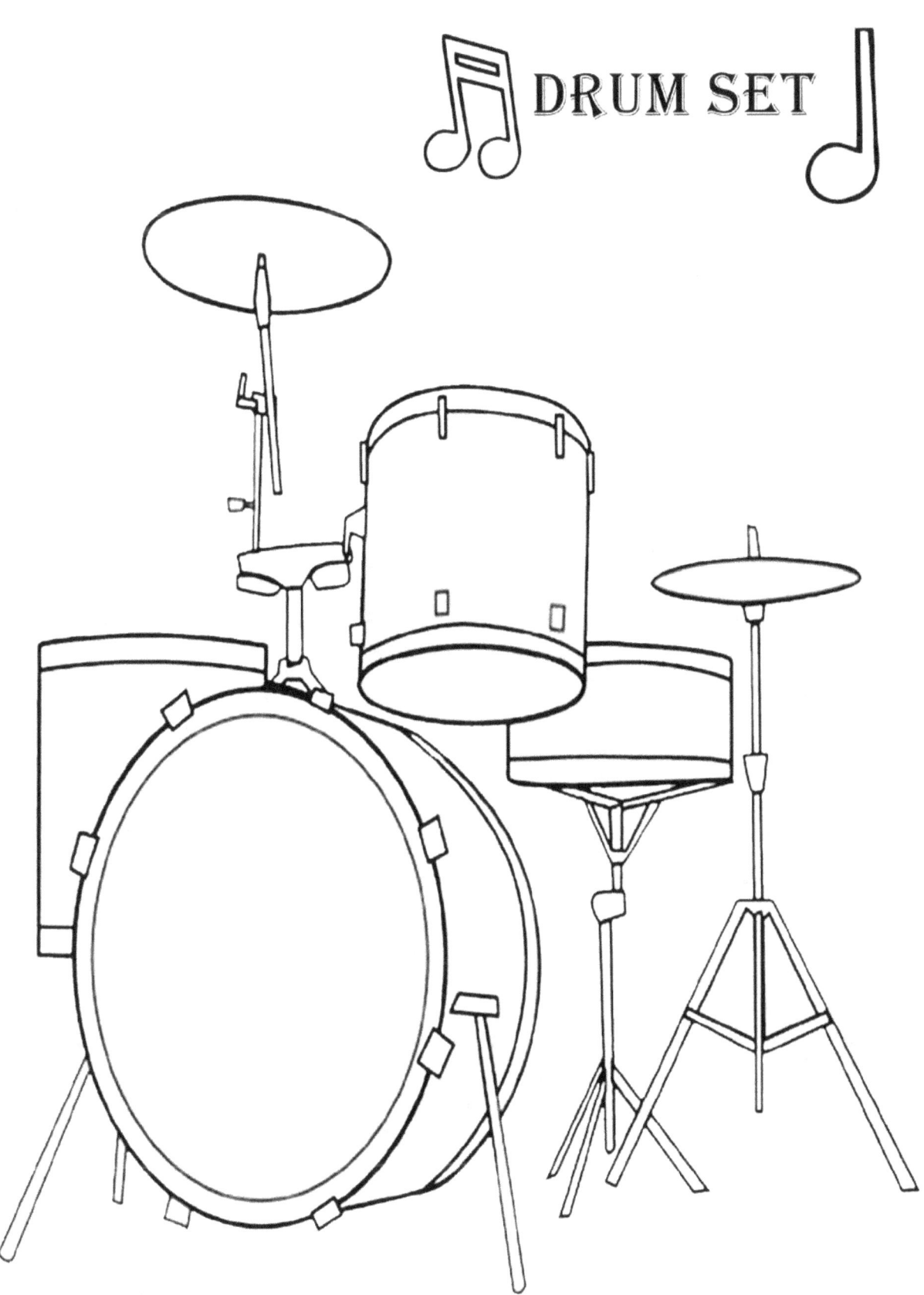

DRUM SET

Drum

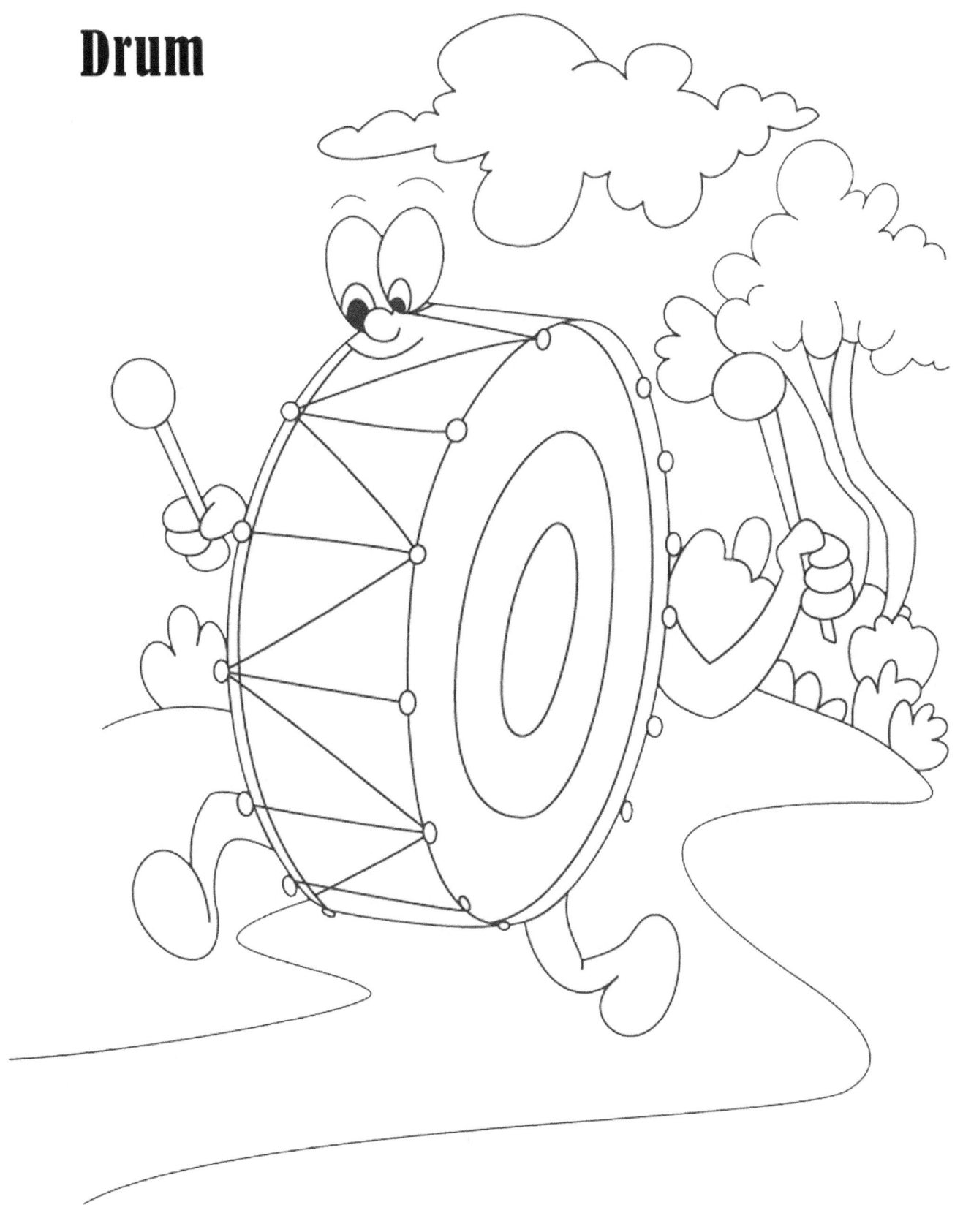

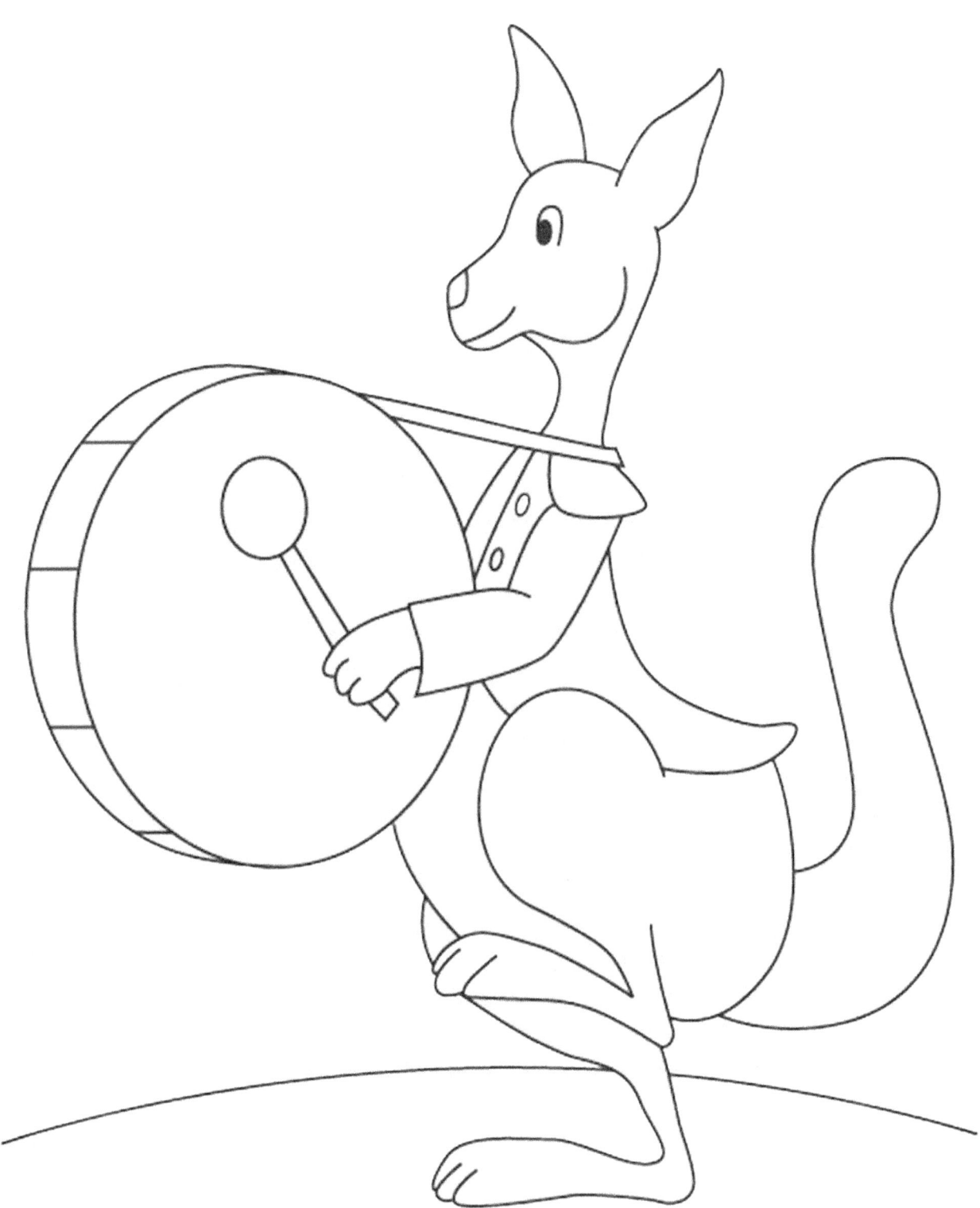

Drum Set

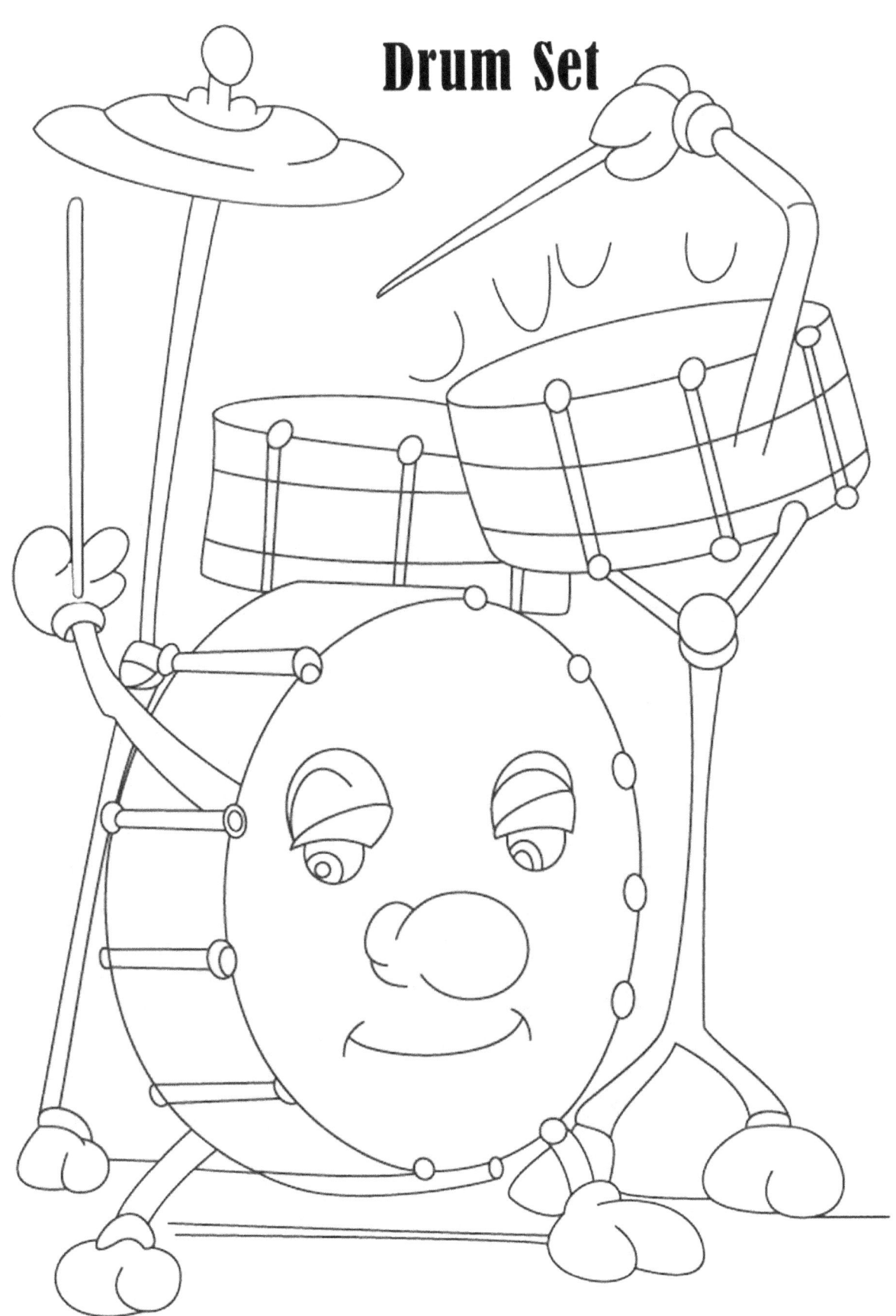

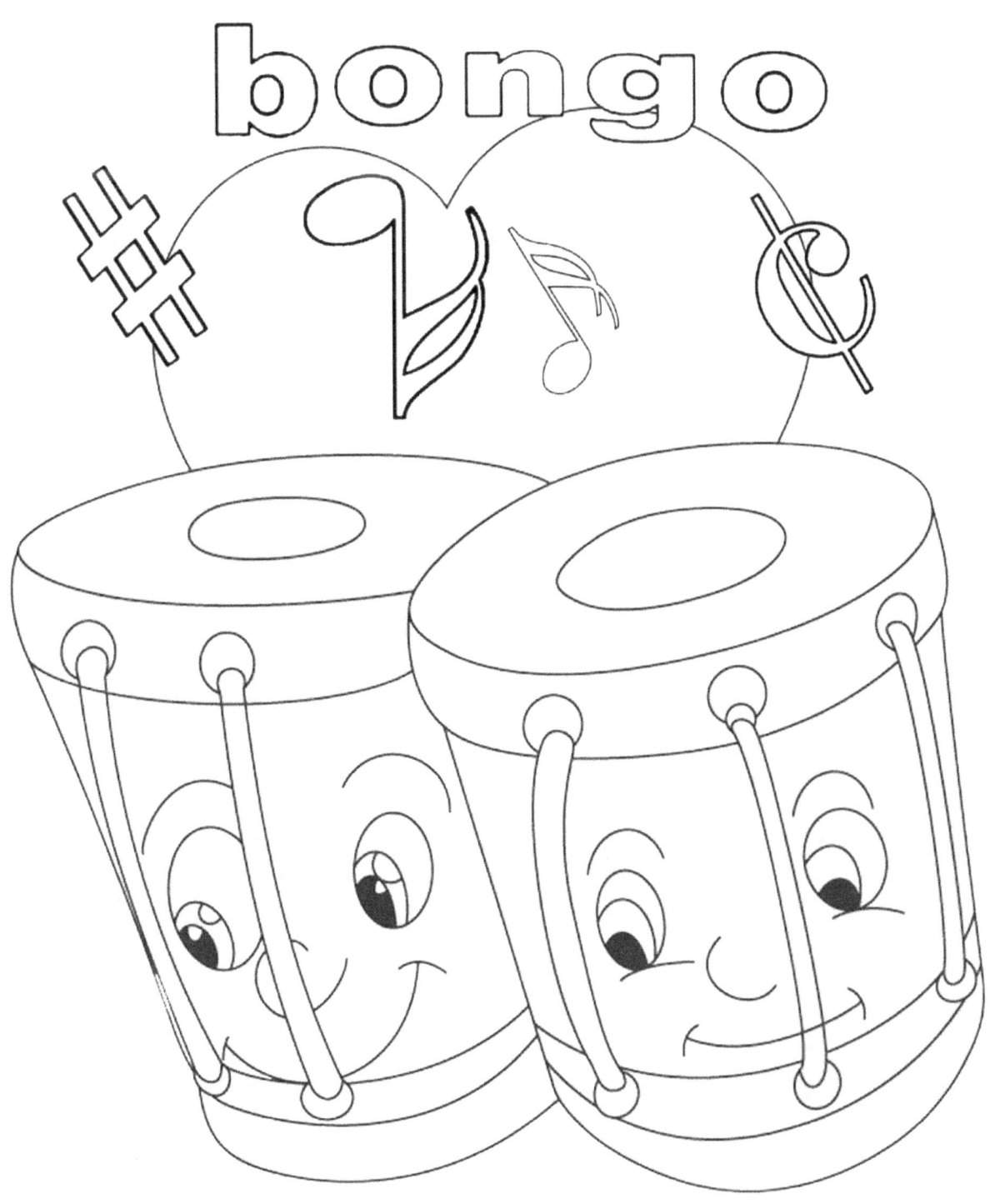

Tabla Drums

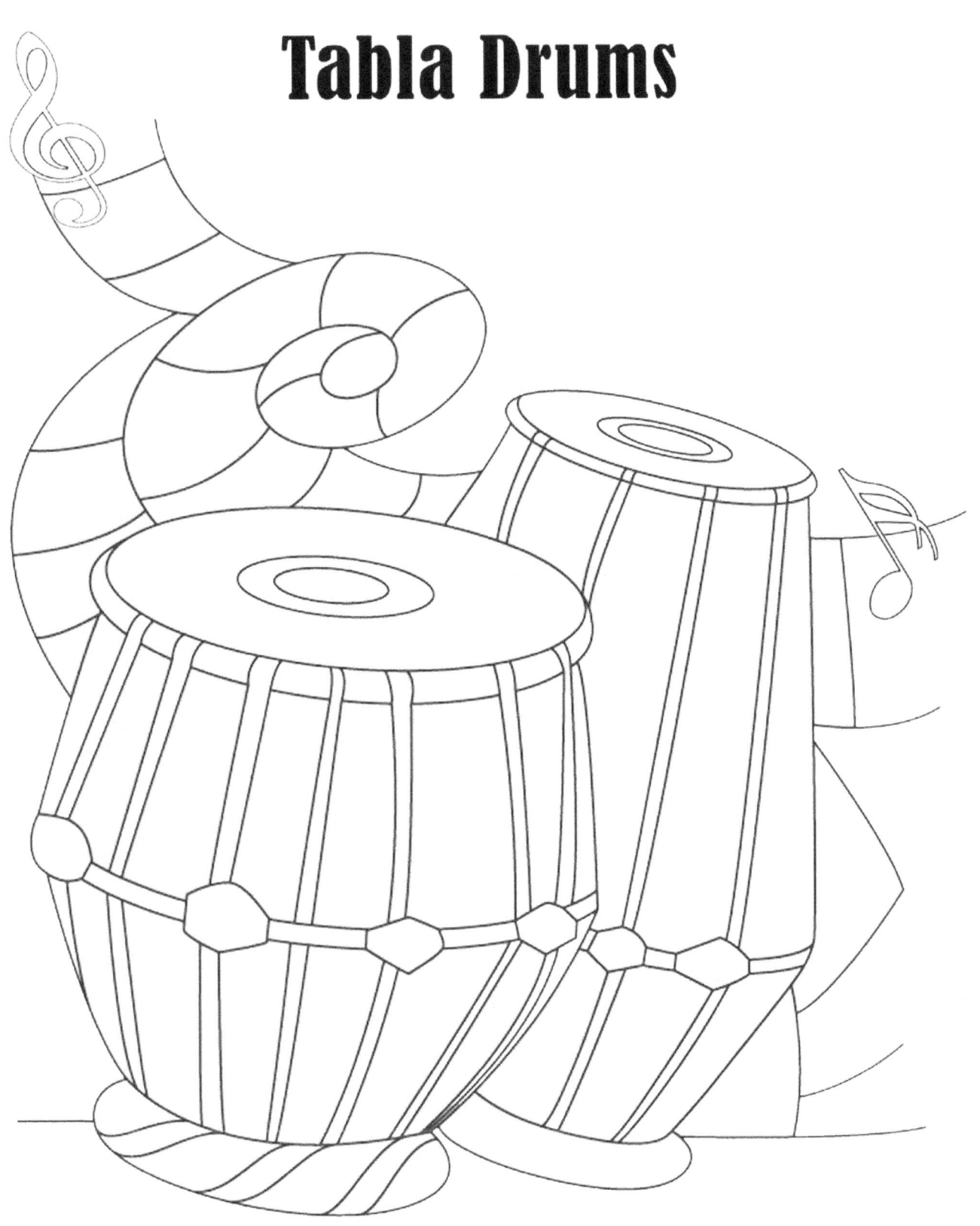

Dholak Indian Drum

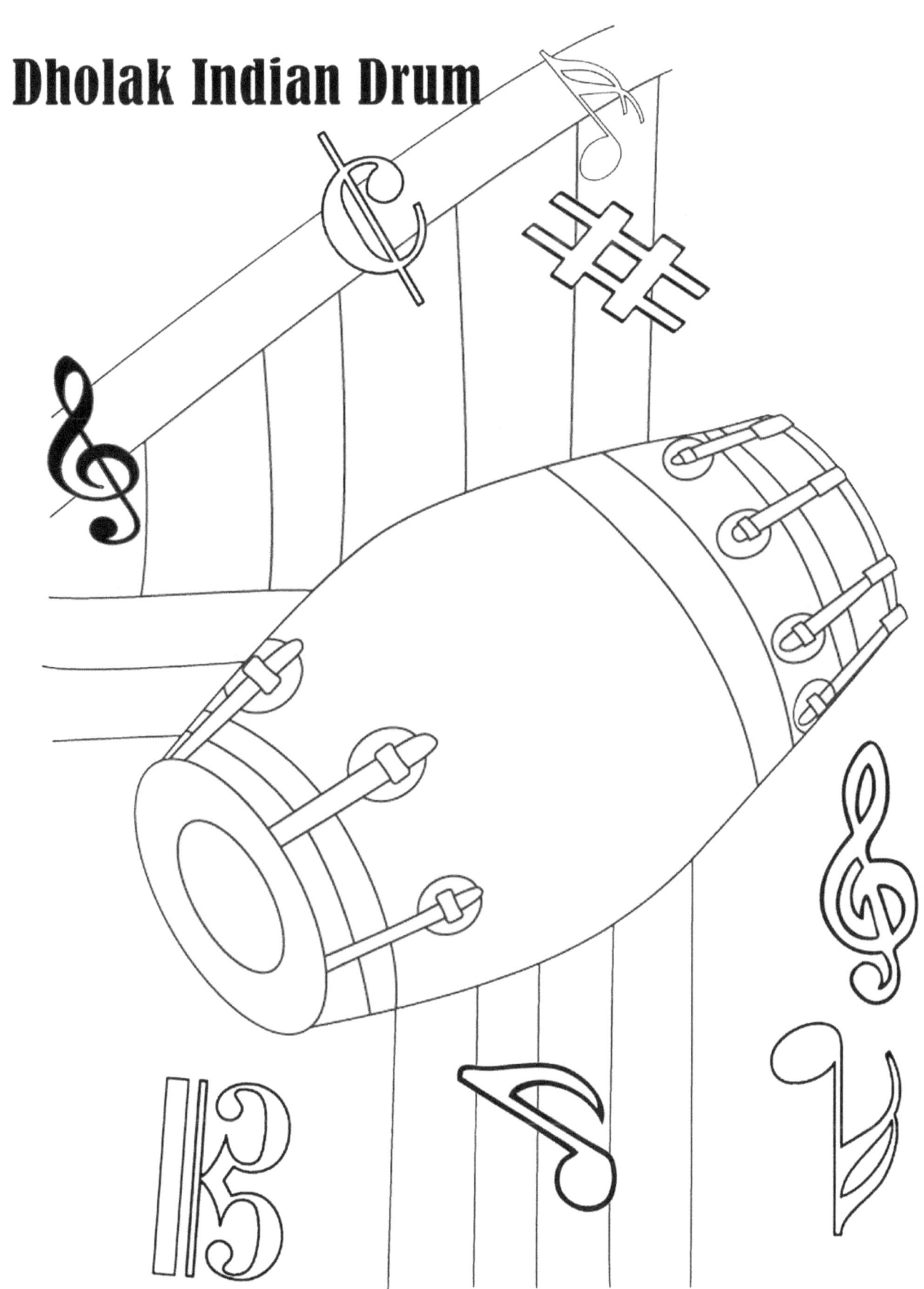

Dholak Indian Drum

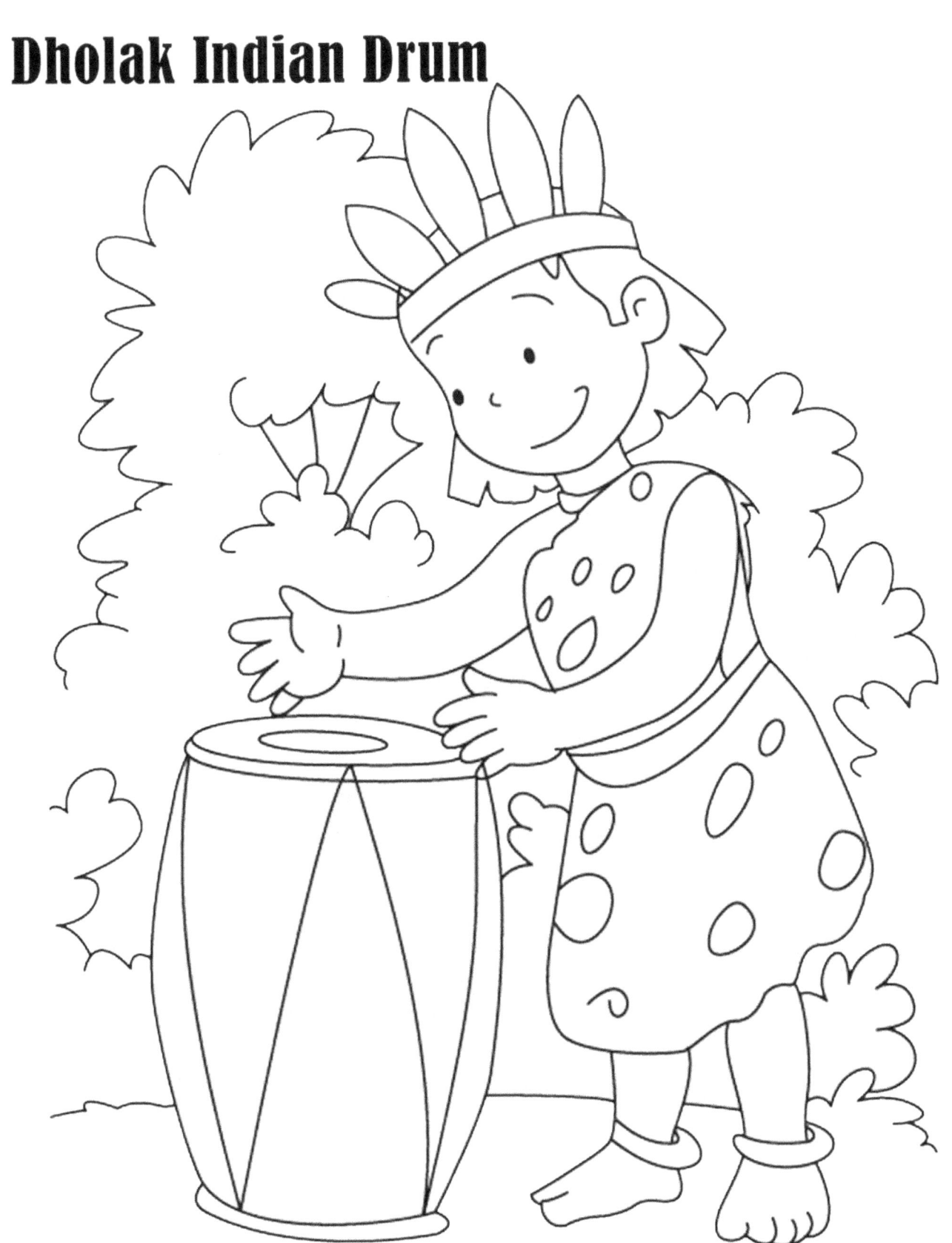

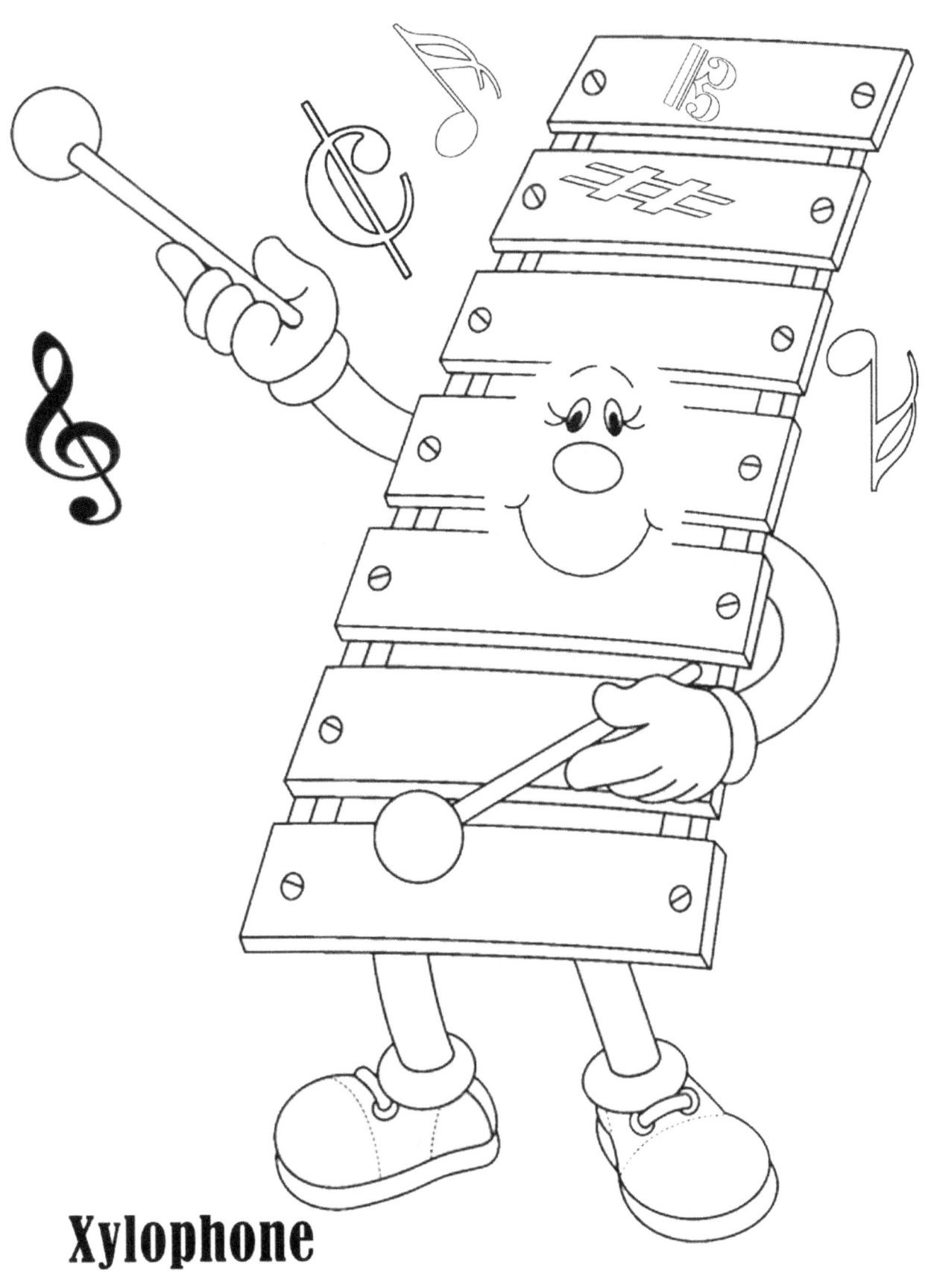

Xylophone

Trumpet

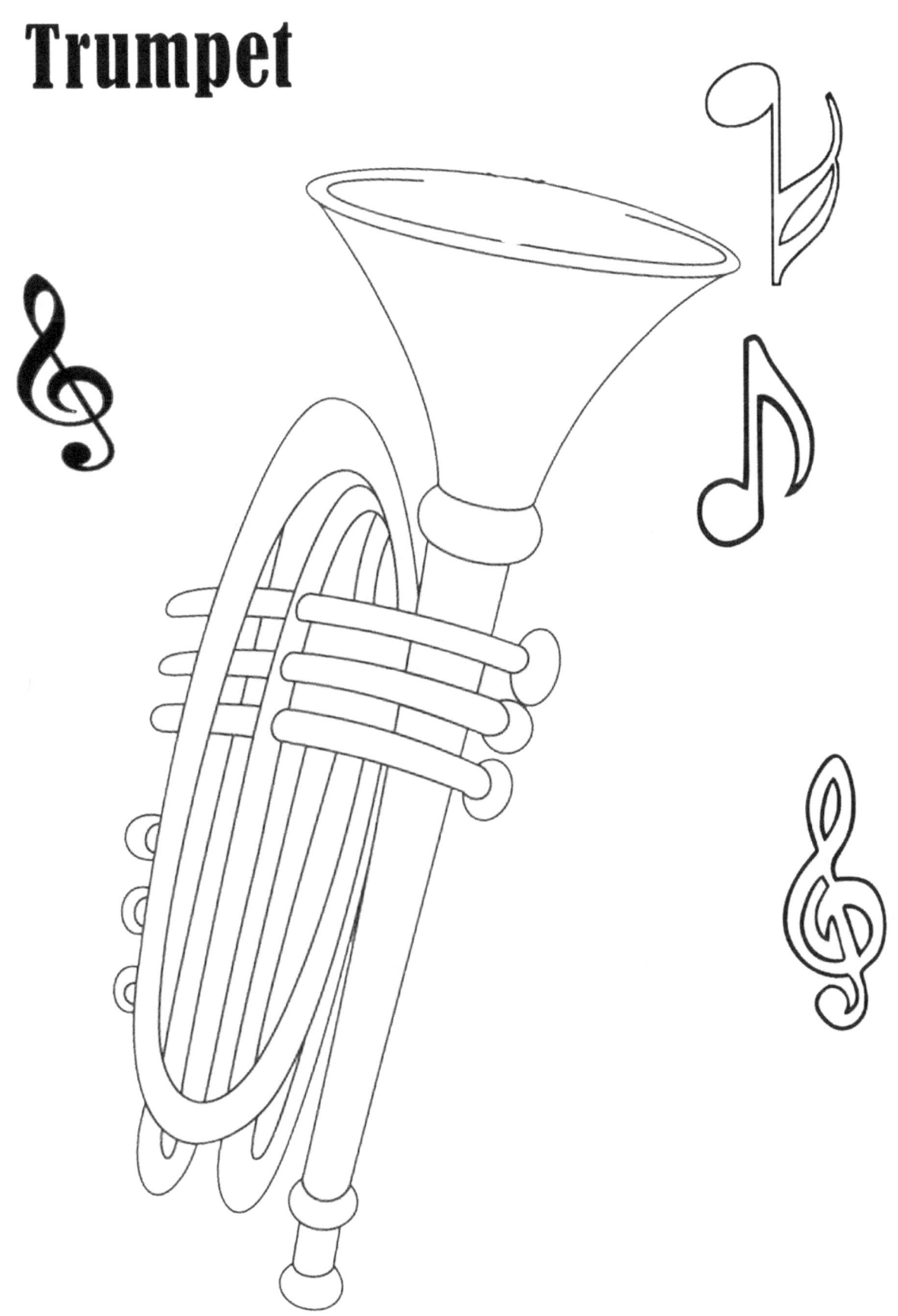

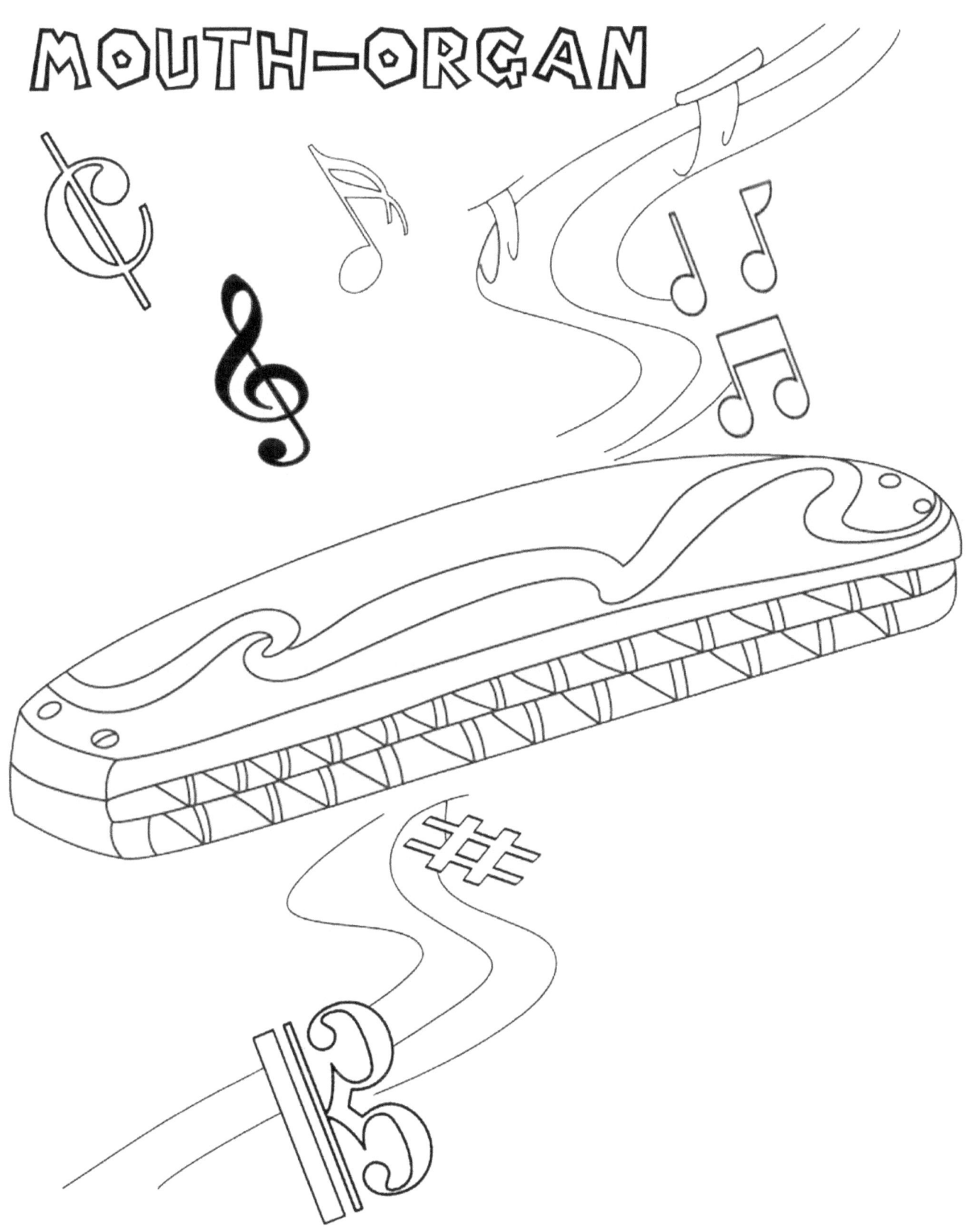

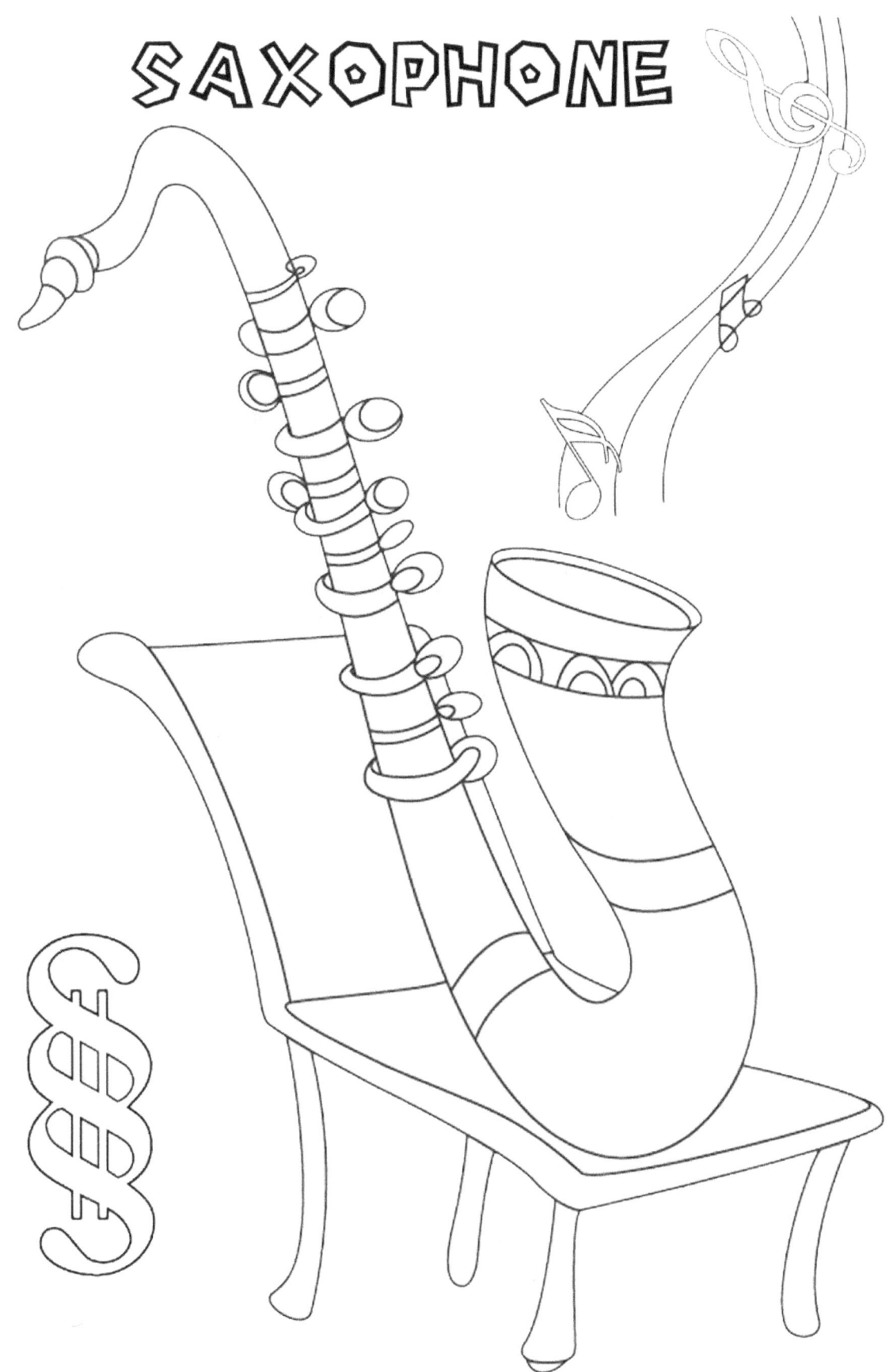

SAXOPHONE

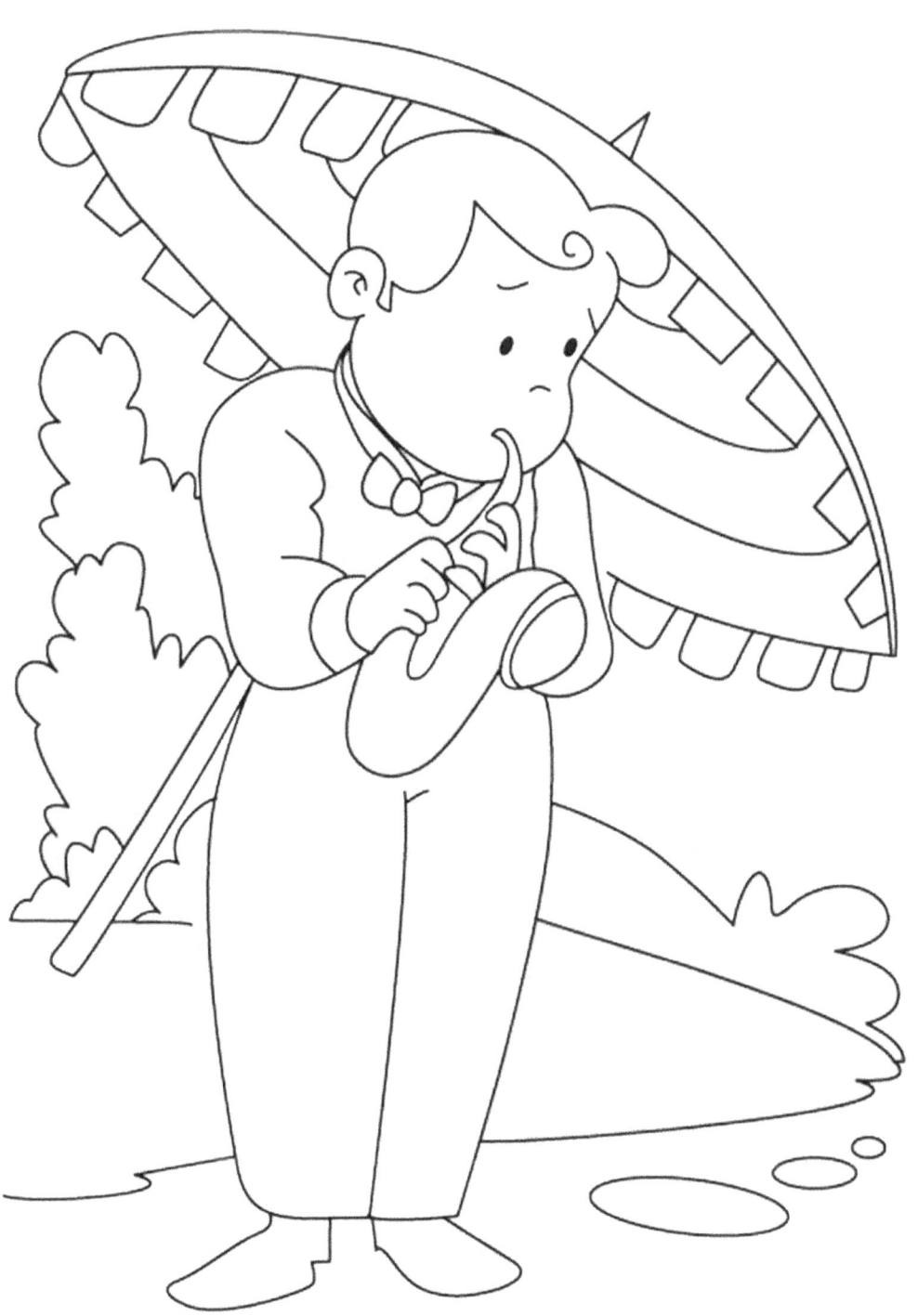

SHEHNAI

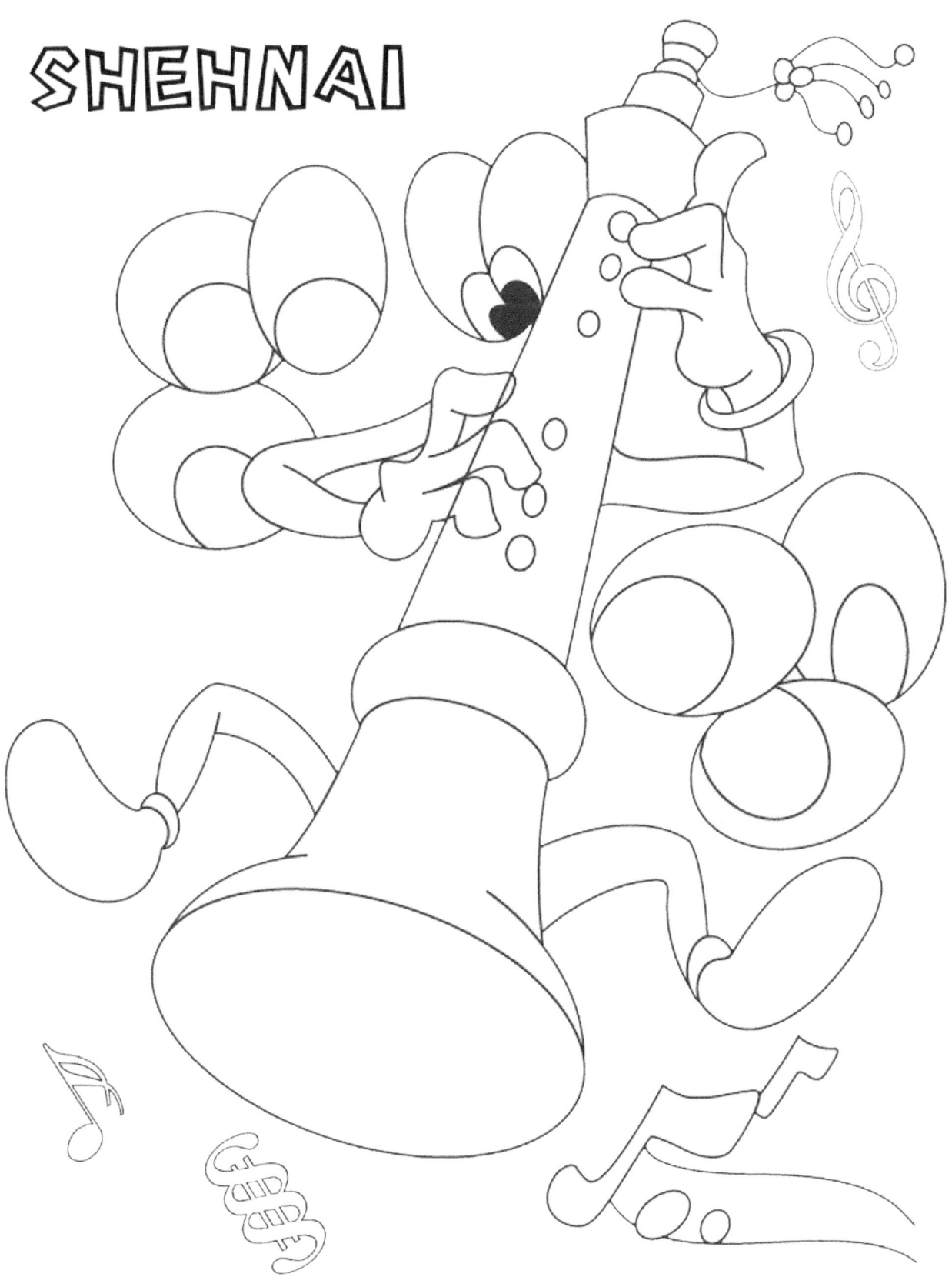

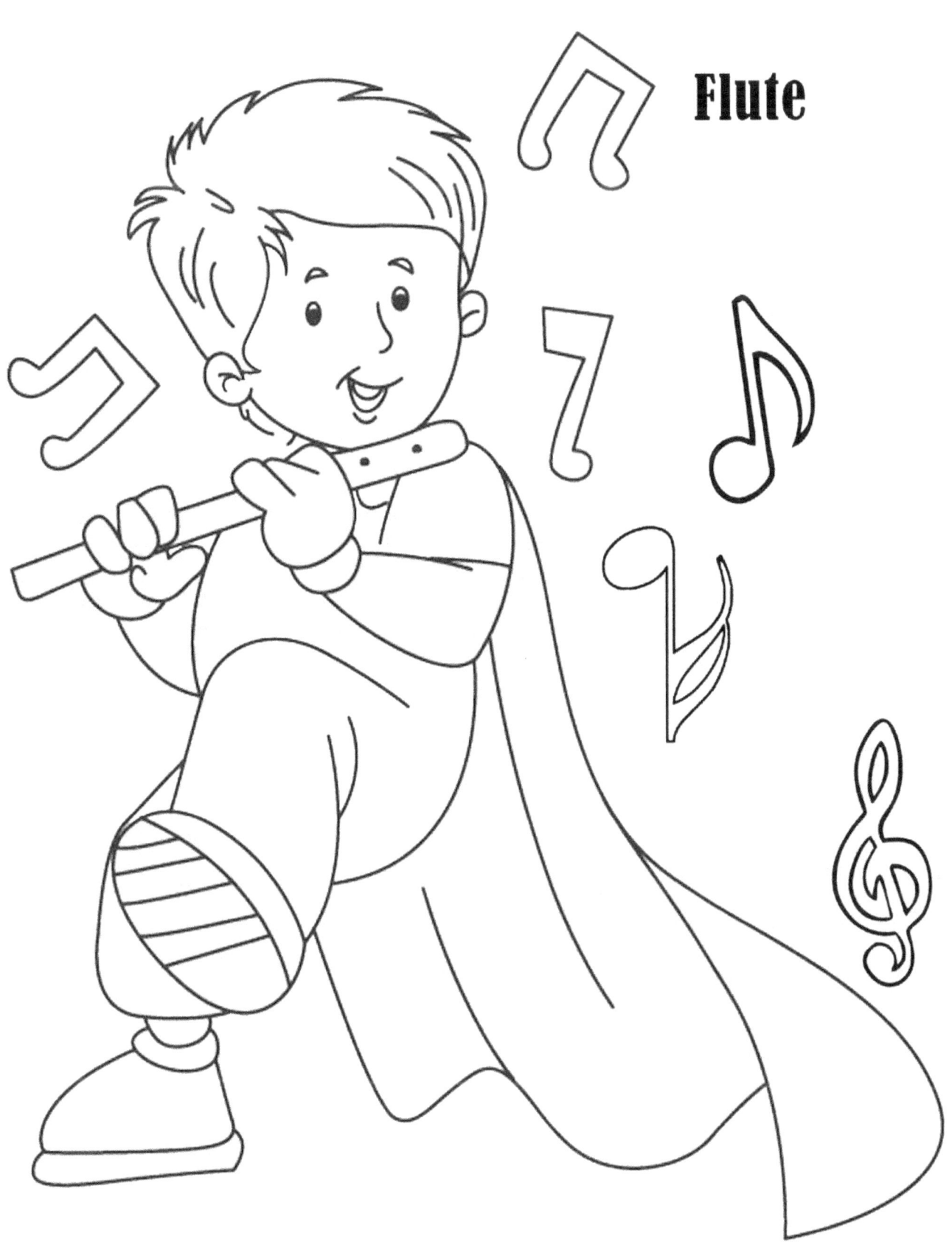

Flute

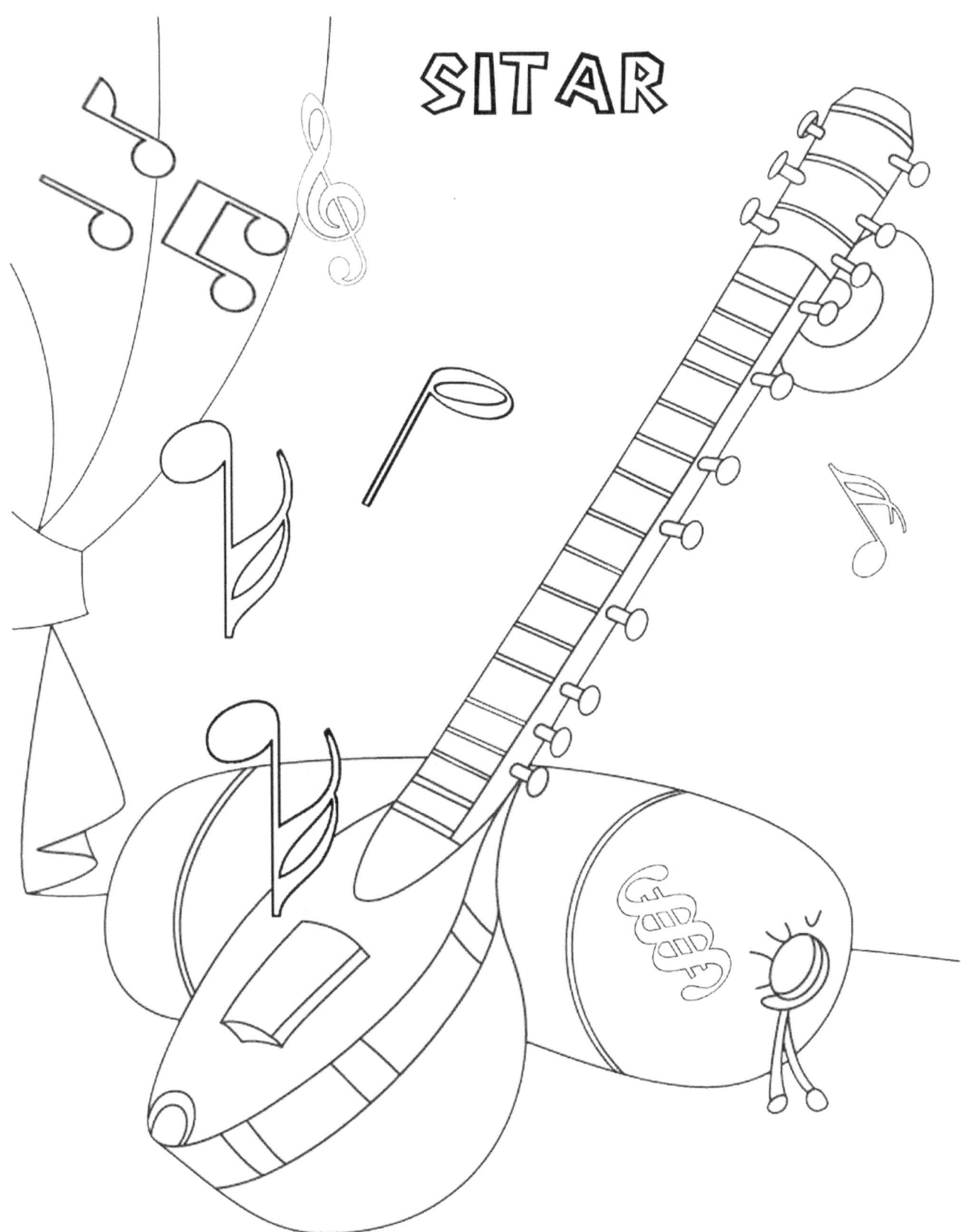

SITAR

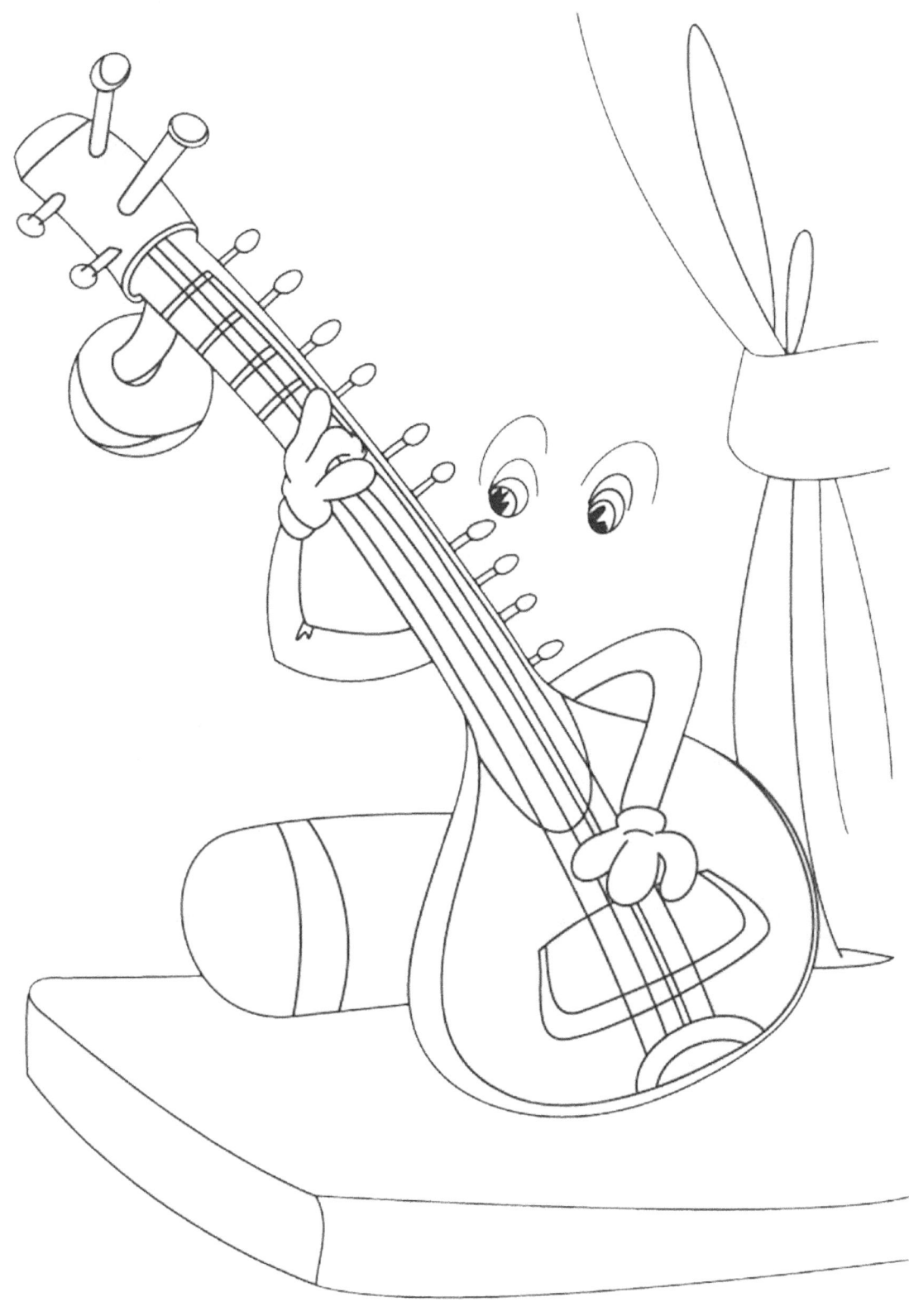

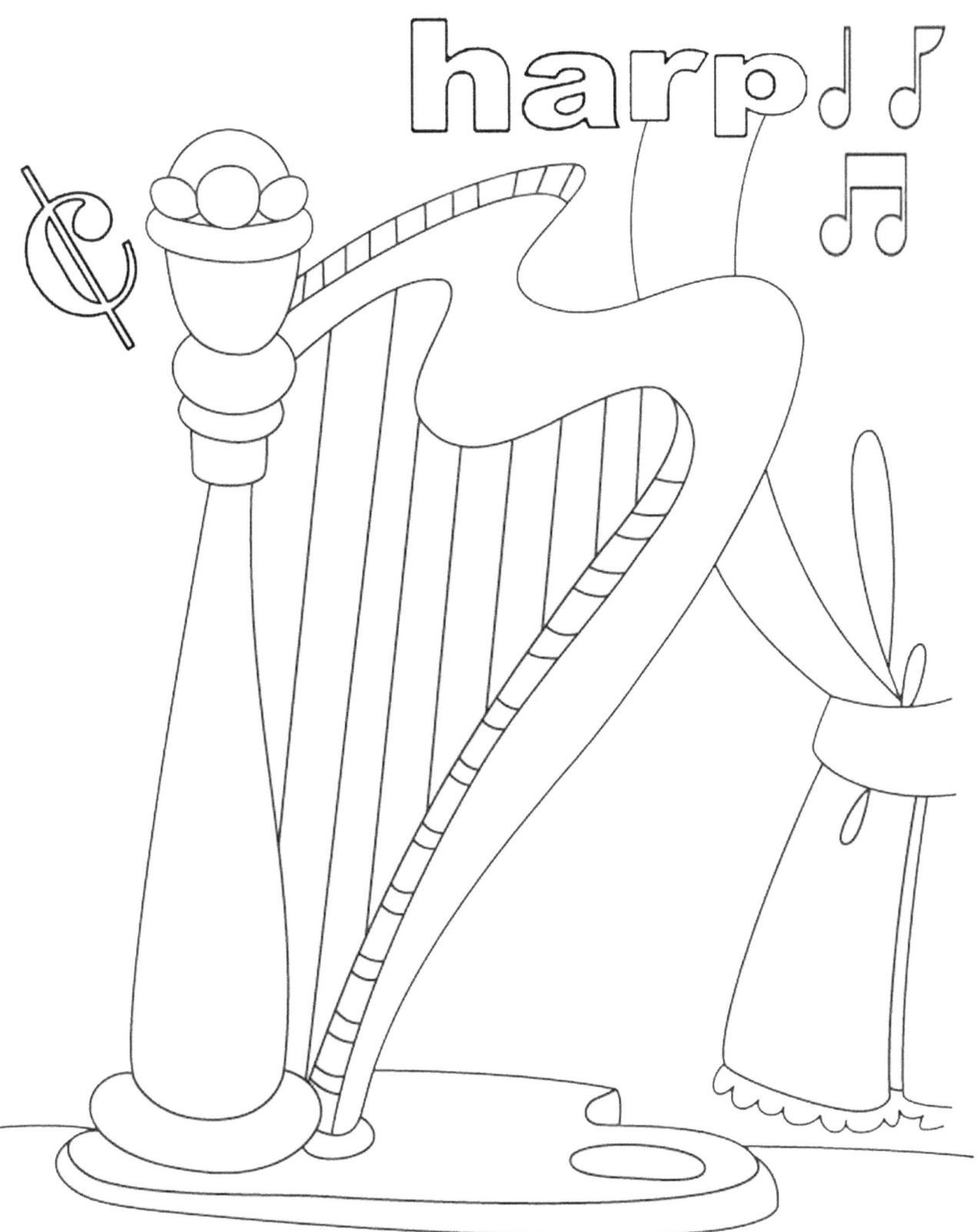

Guitar

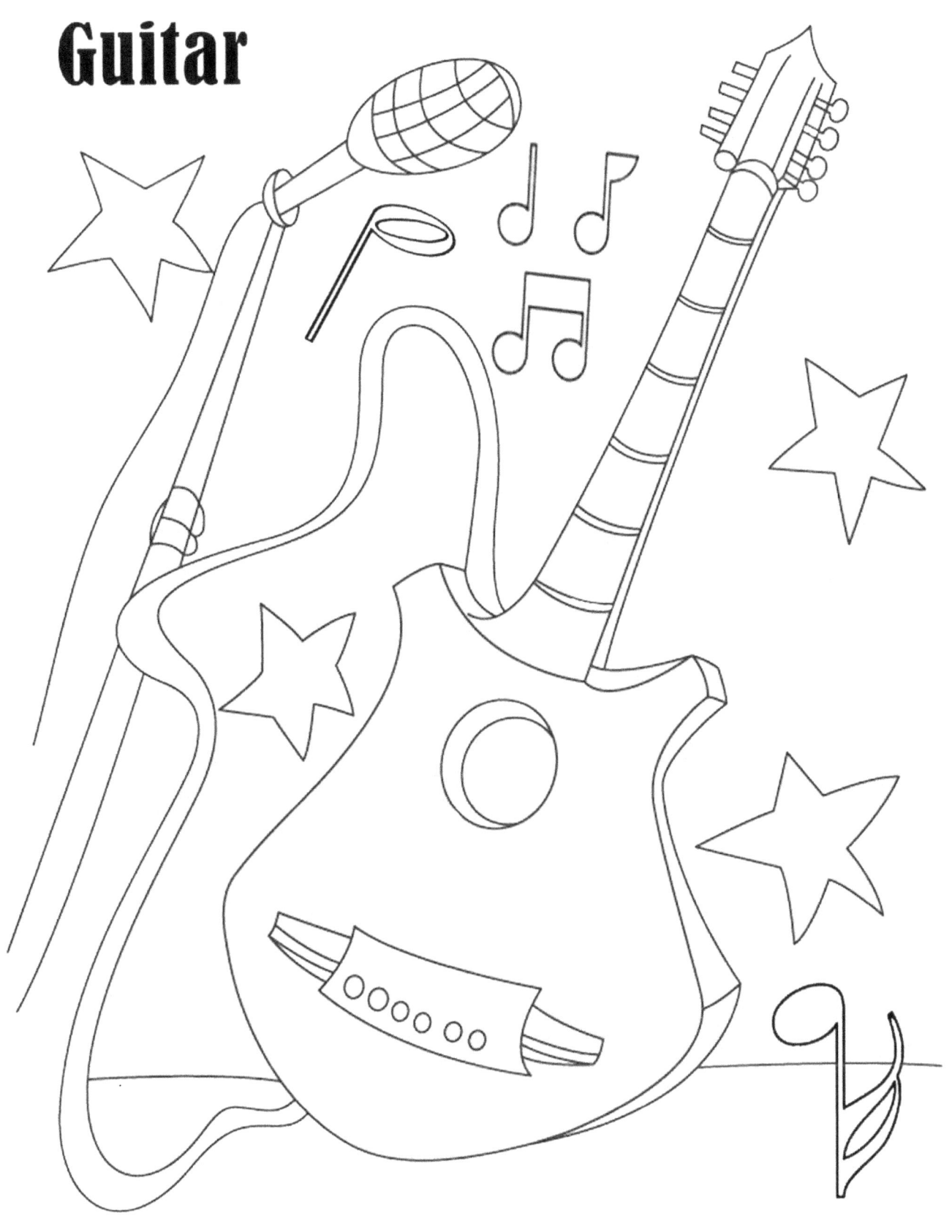

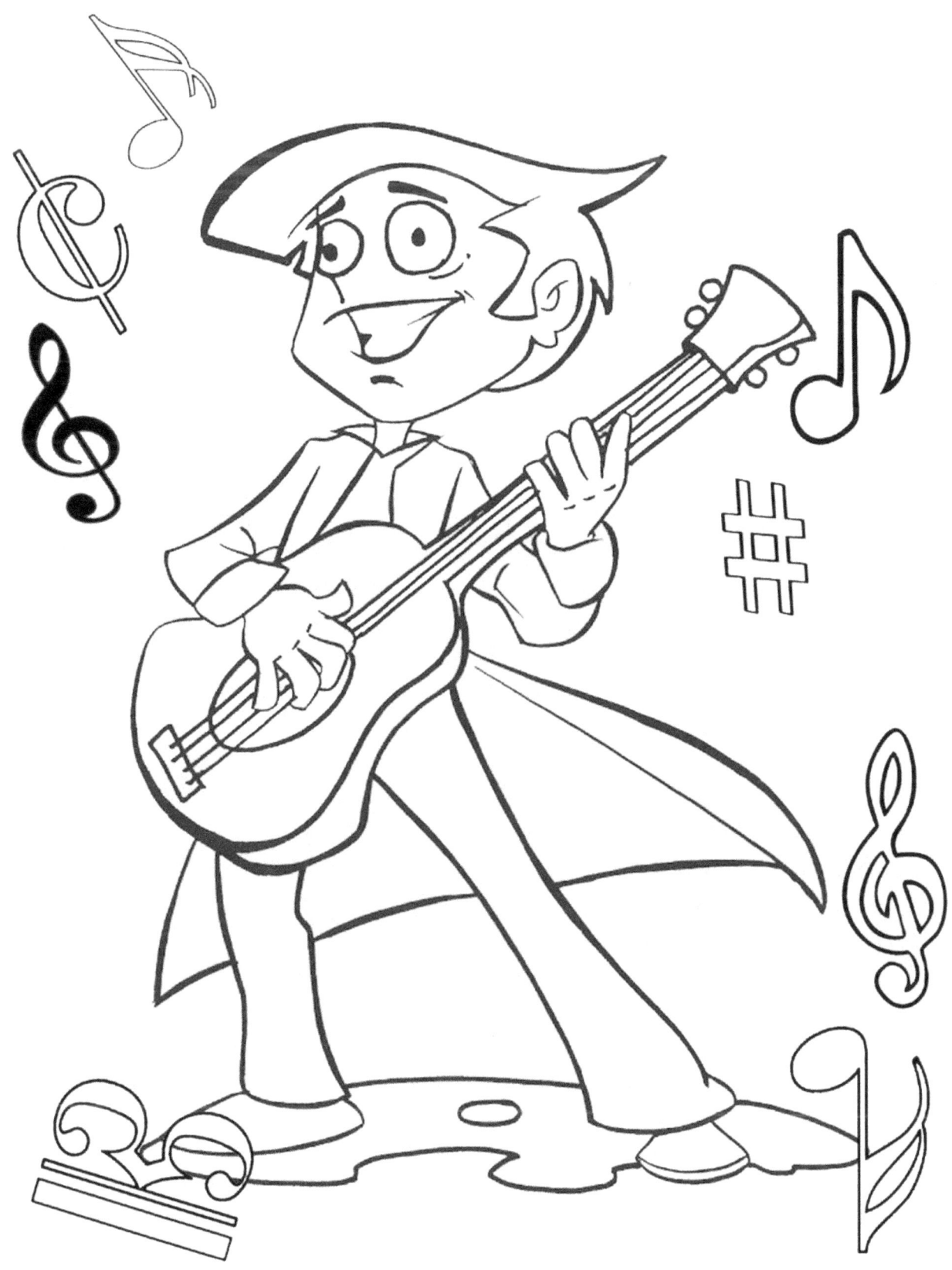

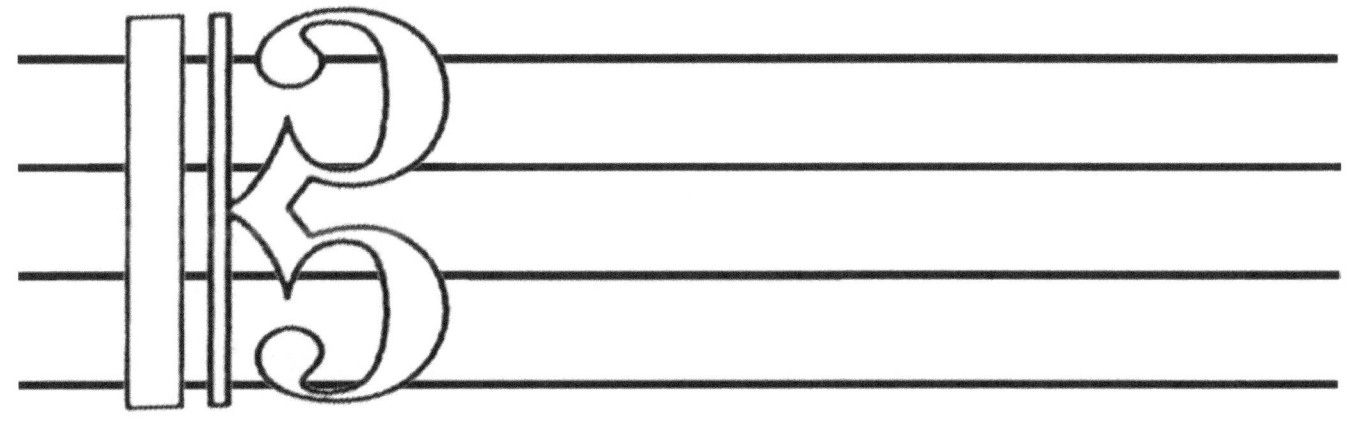

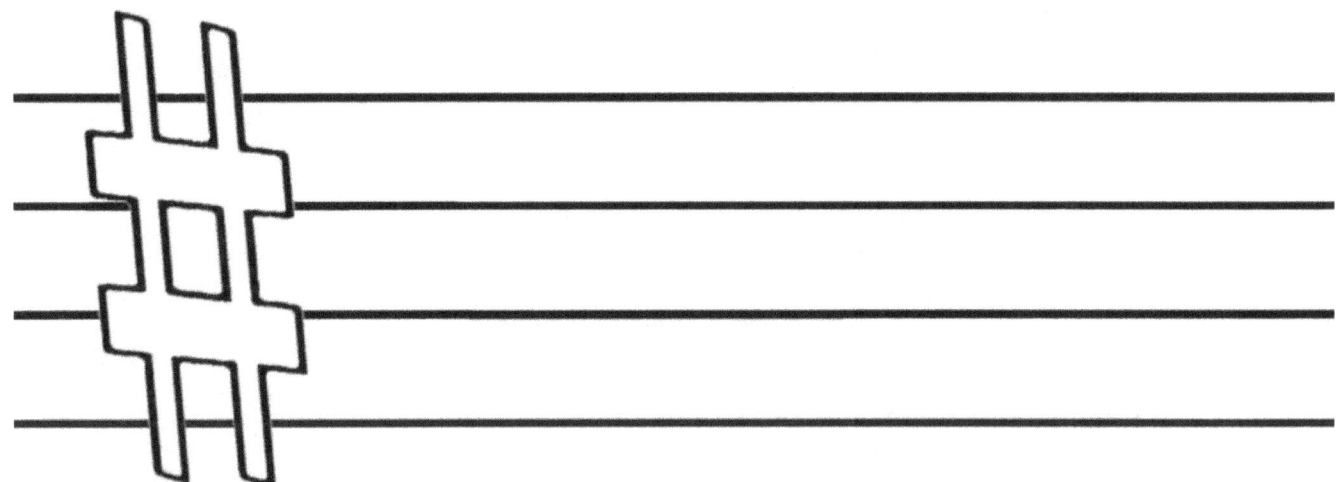

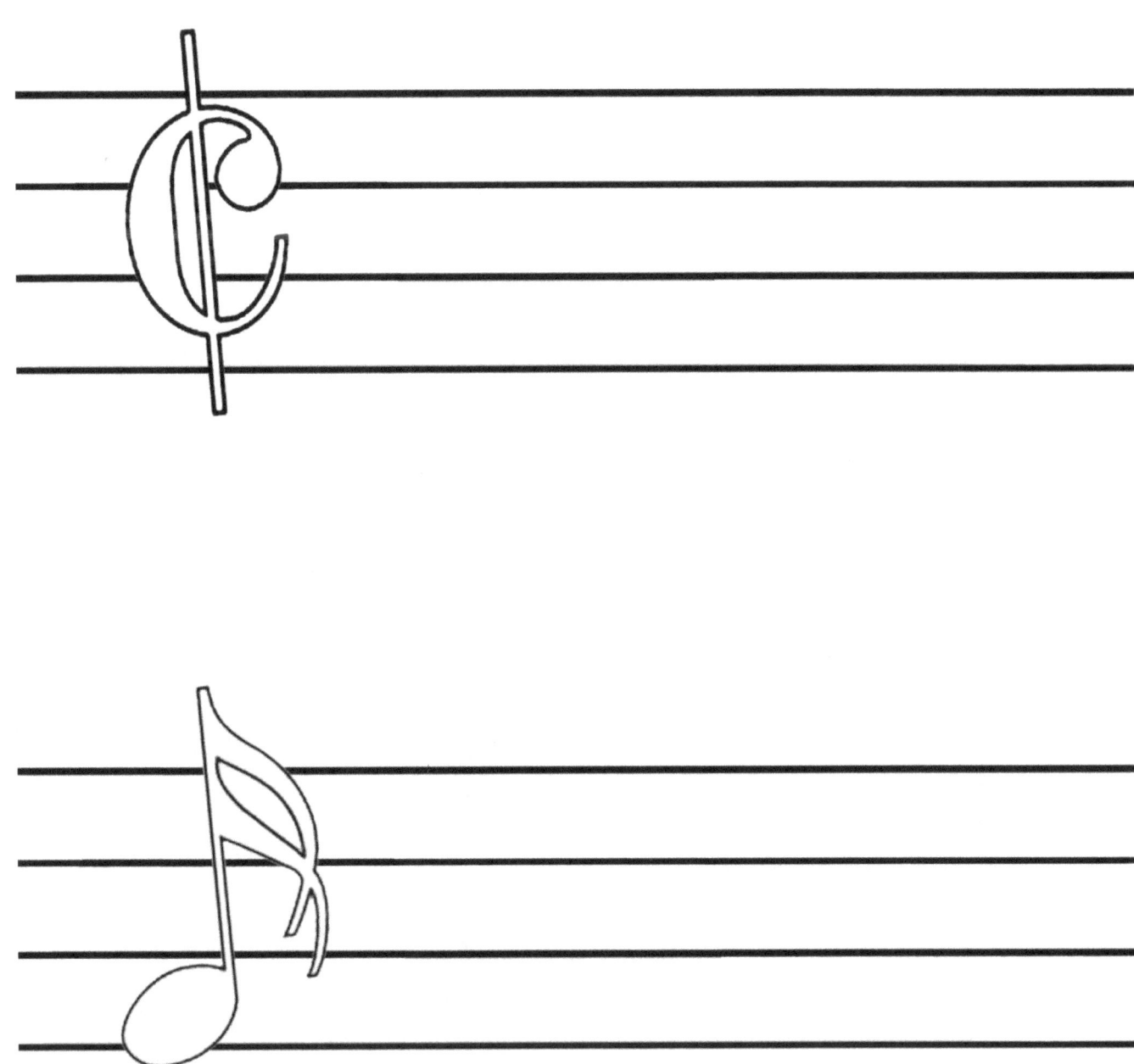

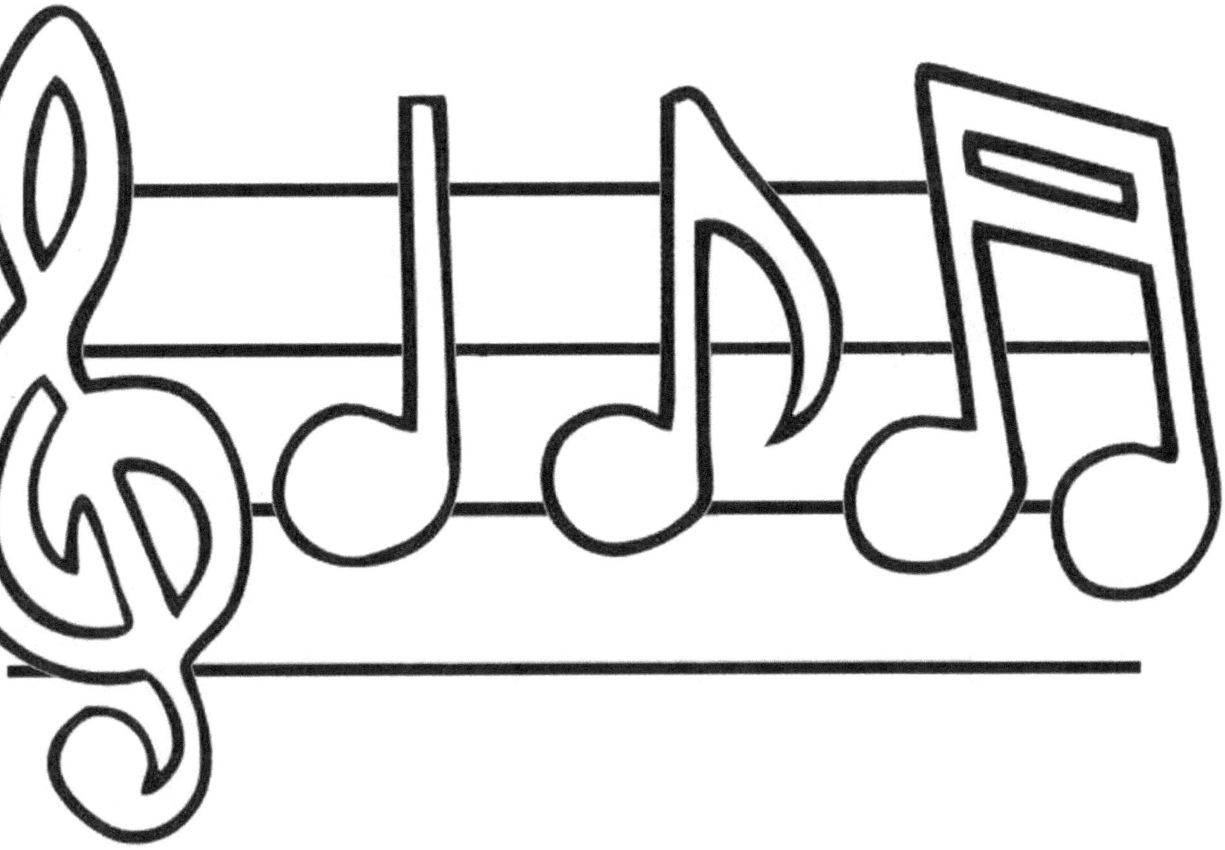

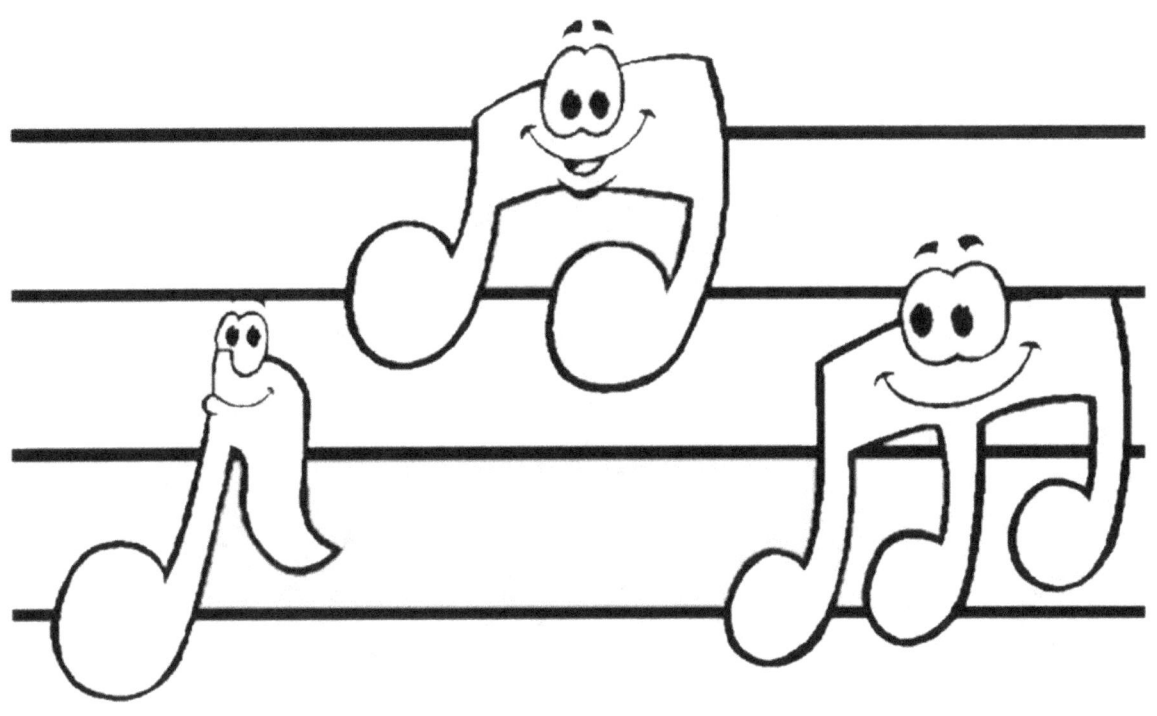

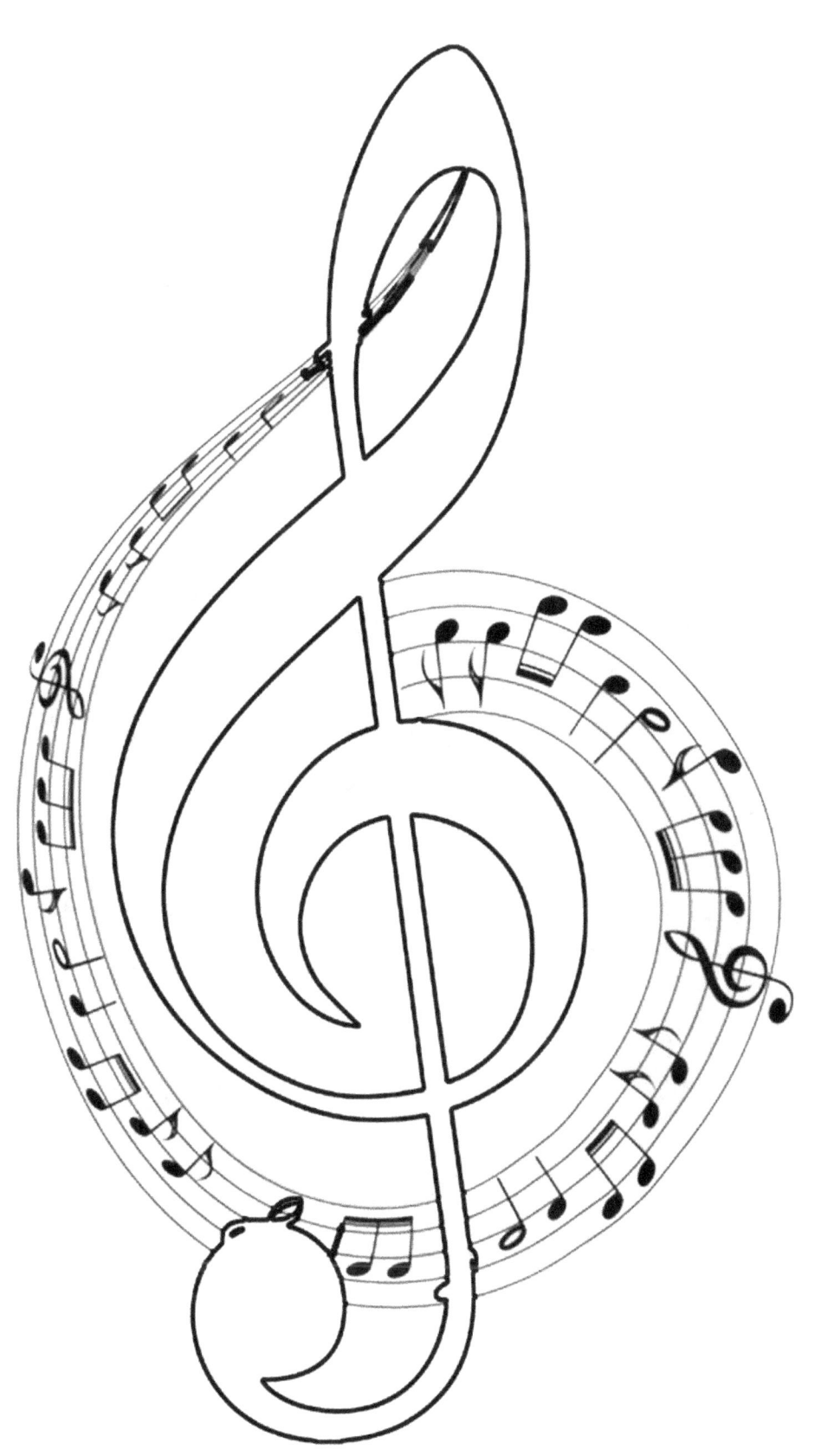

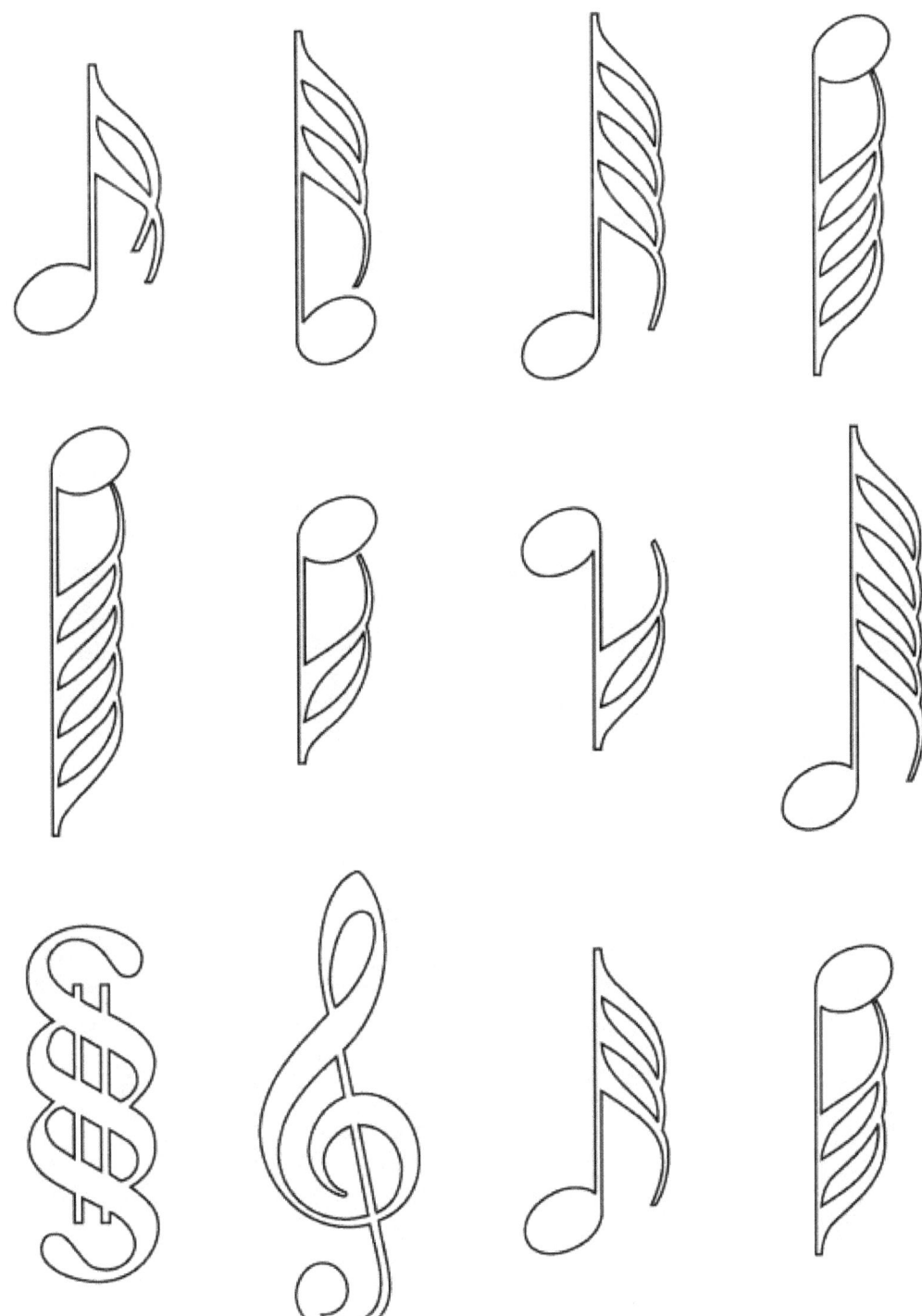

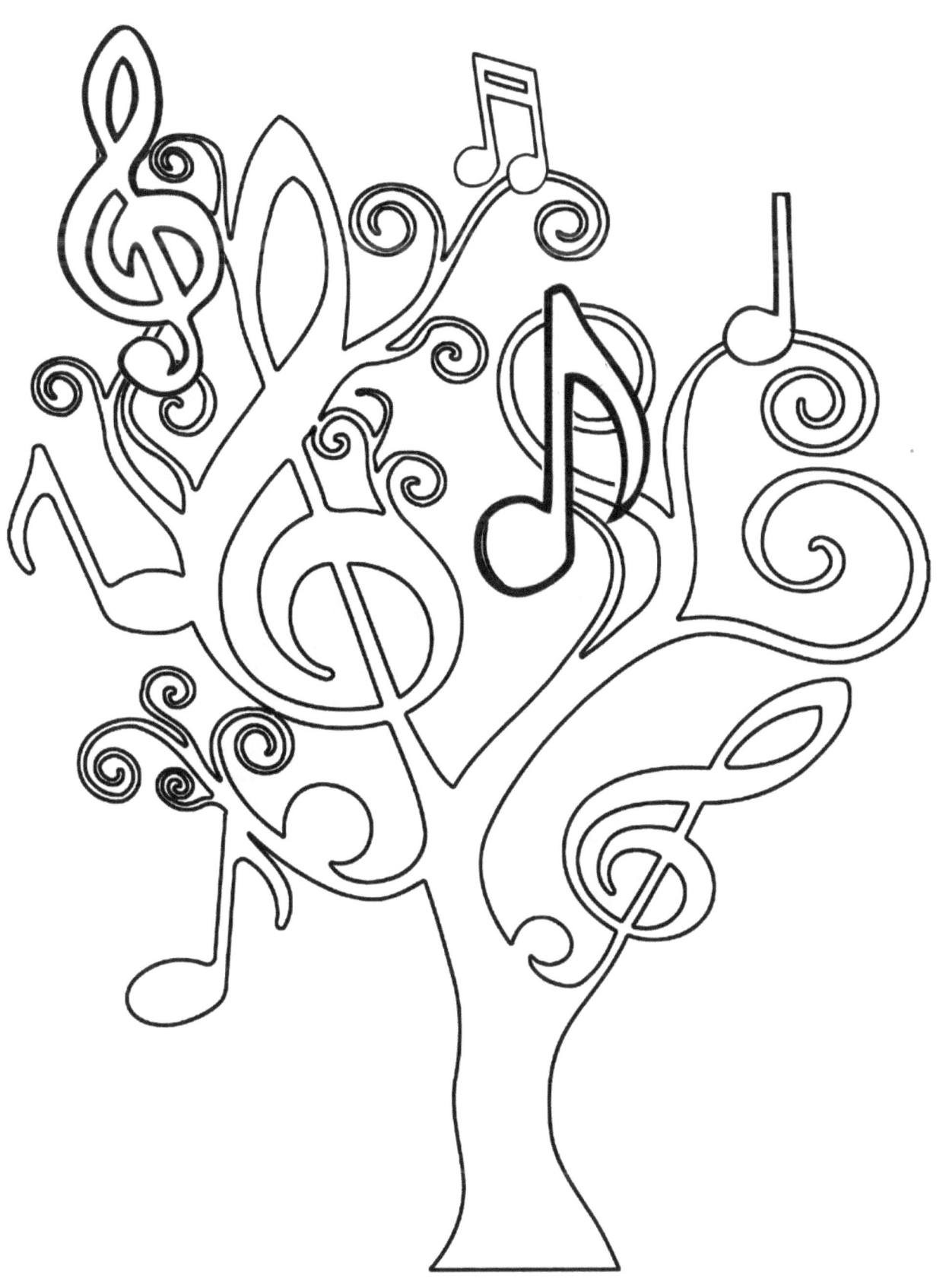

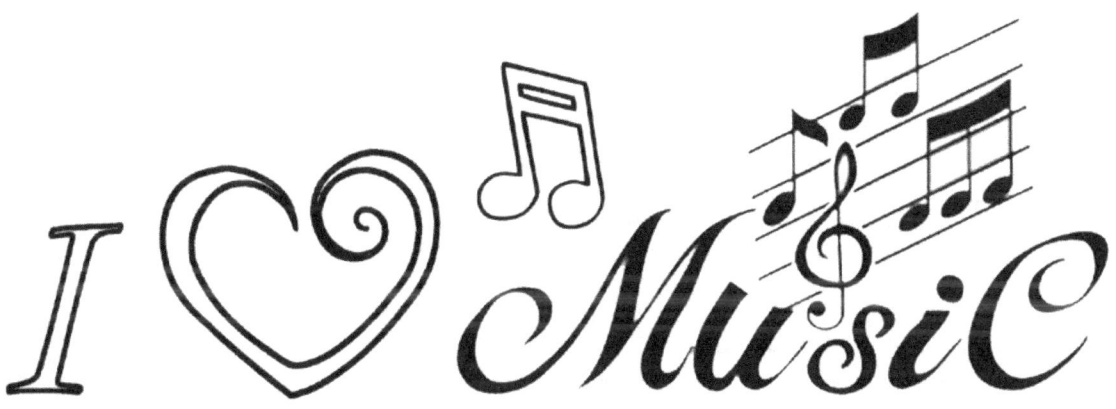

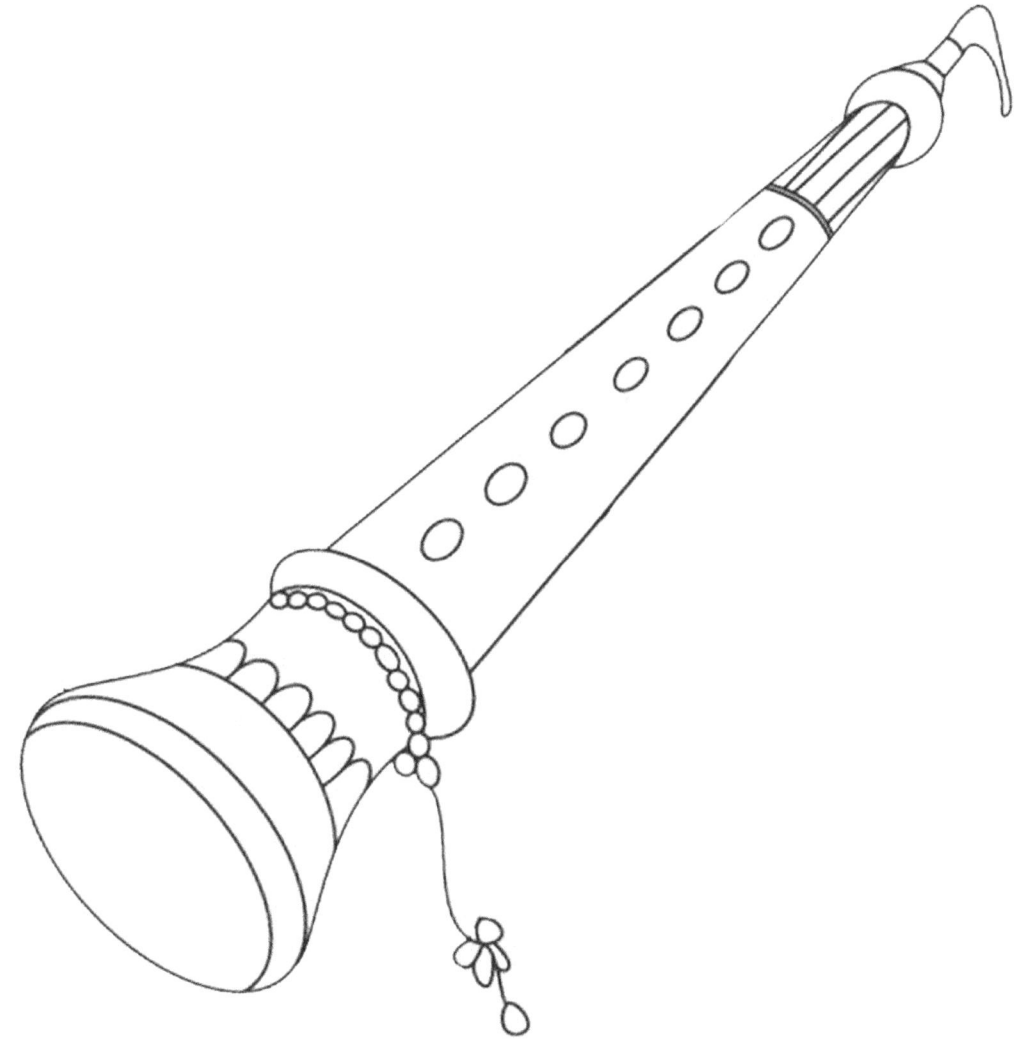

SHEHNAI

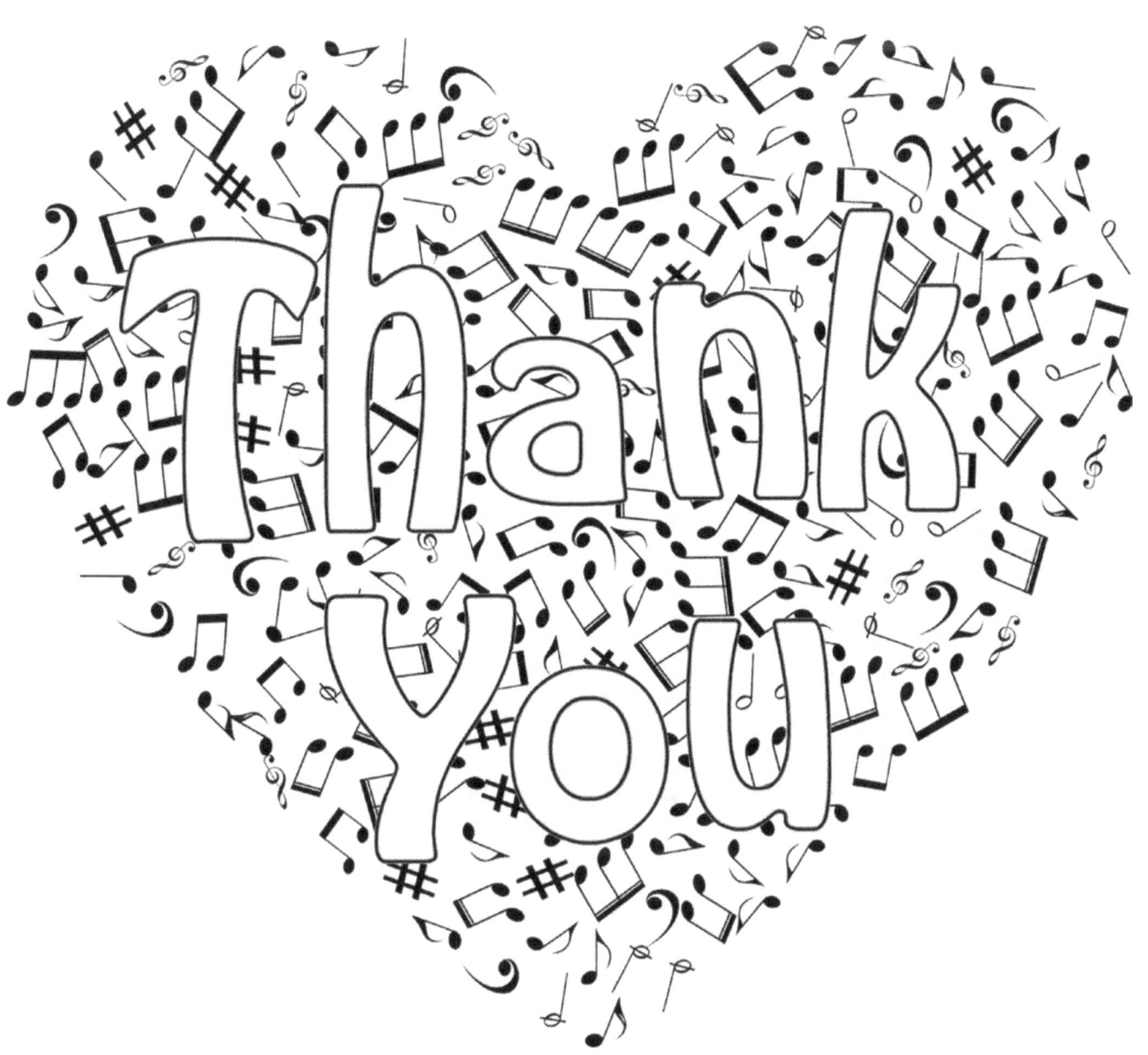